To/ John

Best Wishes

PARALYSIS TO SUCCESS

BOUNCING BACK FROM ADVERSITY

JASON ANKER MBE

Jason Anker

PARALYSIS TO SUCCESS - BOUNCING BACK FROM ADVERSITY
ISBN: 978-1-5272-3434-5

First published in Great Britain
in 2018 through Amazon self-publishing
service Kindle Direct Publishing

To protect the identities of parties that do not with to be named or identitifed; names and locations have been changed by the author.

Permission for W. Mitchell's quote has been granted.
Available at: http://www.wmitchell.com/about/

Produced by samanthahoughton.co.uk

In Memory of Dan Terry, a Safety Visionary
08/06/1964 - 09/07/2018
'Be the change you want to see in the world'

Contents

Acknowledgments

Writing this book was harder than I thought and more rewarding than I could have ever imagined. None of this would have been possible without the continued help and support from my family and friends.

I'm eternally grateful to my Mum and Dad, their love, support and help never waivered even in my darkest times.

To my sister Sharon for always being the person I could turn to during those dark and desperate years.

My, now grown up children, Abbi and Sam, bringing you up brought me so much happiness and gave me focus on what really matters.

For Elle, my beautiful granddaughter who brings me so much joy.

A very special thanks to all my family and amazing friends who there are too many to name individually as with my shocking memory I'm bound to forget someone and cause offence.

Finally, to all those who have been a part of my getting there especially since I started presenting, 'My Story.' To Dan Terry, who was the one who initially encouraged me to start talking in the first place and who mentored me, Matt Terry, who also gave me great guidance and still does today and now to Prof Tim Marsh, not just for the advice over the years but now as a business partner. Thank you to all the work clients and contacts that I have not just worked with but have also became great friends with. It is because of their efforts and encouragement that I have a legacy to pass on to my family where one didn't exist before.

Writing a book about the story of your life is a surreal process. I'm forever indebted to Sam Houghton for her ghostwriting, advice, help, keen insight, and ongoing support in bringing my story to life.

Testimonials

"I've been with this company now for more years than I care to remember, and within that time I've listened to, and been to, a thousand and one or more safety presentations done by the company, SHE dept. etc. But none that I've been to comes anywhere near, in putting a safety message across as this one did. As soon as I got back to my place of work I let everyone know about Jason Anker's story. His message certainly hit home." - Dave -NAS Welder

"As an apprentice when I started with the company I undertook an induction, before having a local induction. Having been asked to attend the Jason Anker presentation I didn't know what to expect, and to be honest his presentation was educational, emotional and funny. Educational certainly as we all learnt from Jason's mistakes, I will always take '5' before climbing a ladder. The emotional side comes from listening to what Jason had been through, and the path his life's taken. The funny side was how Jason put it in his own words and he himself added humour. During his presentation I took several glances behind me noticing everyone giving Jason their full attention. I certainly took Jason Anker's message back to the workplace." - Aysha - Apprentice Sheet Metal Worker

"I believe Jason touched and captivated the audience within a few minutes of starting. Jason told his story with intimate details of his private life, when he talked about the difficult experiences he went through with his family, it became very emotional because he was sharing every single detail of his struggle following his accident. Overall the presentation was very successful with a good impact on safety culture, and afterwards on the shop floor I noticed some changes in relation to work at height from one individual" - Chris -SHEQ Manager

"A Lasting impression... Along with everyone in the audience, I was absorbed as Jason told us of his life before the incident and then described the day of the incident in detail. He spoke of the highs and the lows since that day, such as time spent in hospital and rehabilitation, his release from hospital and his struggle with life over the past 22 years and the effect the incident has had on his family and friends. Jason's presentation is more powerful than any I can ever make, and the message is very simple - every single one of us has a choice to make about being safe, (or unsafe) at work, and we bear responsibility for the consequences." - Dame Judith Hackitt

"I just wanted to say to Jason and his friend Sean what a fantastic way of getting over to us all about safety, and of course the aspects of just a few seconds out of life and the impact on all lives around the injured, or even, sadly, dead party. I am a Health & Safety Rep on site so get involved more than some, and for me I went through a one and half hour emotional roller coaster. Jason puts his story over so plainly, bluntly, amusingly, and emotionally, but so effectively it's amazing. My breaking point was the video of his parents, at that point I almost left the room for fear of sobbing loudly but managed to keep myself in check. Please pass on my personal thanks to him for the work he and Sean do to promote safety, not only at work but in our lives as a whole." - Janice

Prologue

There's something beautiful to be said about broken fragments of ceramics that are pieced together and repaired with lacquer dusted with gold. In Japan this is an ancient art known as "kintsugi," which translates as golden joinery. It treats these breakages as a part of the object's history and which is lovingly put back together and celebrated rather than be seen as something to be disguised.

This can be likened to how a person can describe as feeling "broken" after experiencing traumatic life events such as grief, heartbreak or illnesses. Rather than their shattered selves being hidden or viewed as taboo, maybe they too can be encouraged to embrace any imperfections and vulnerabilities. The strength within the breakage is what makes the person and their life's journey so interesting and uniquely incredible.

*This book may trigger anyone whom has experienced trauma

1
The Break Up

Home was Southwell, near Newark, and at a vulnerable yet resilient, four years old, my little world changed overnight. I loved my mum and dad dearly and we had such a happy home but when they both announced they were not going to be together anymore that day, a part of me remembers feeling torn. They both explained it to me in a manner that I understood in my little mind at the time. I loved them both with equal measures and they made me feel secure and loved but I just wasn't sure how I would be able to share myself without one of them feeling left out somehow. It did bother me a little and I remember that time of feeling confused.

My older sister, Sharon and older brother, David, both chose to live with my dad, Keith. As they were considerably older than me, at ten and seven years my senior, they were settled at their schools and with their friendship groups. I was still a baby really, at four years old and at that stage where you "belong with your mum." My mum, June, had found someone else she wanted to spend her life with, and Fred, fast became a huge part of my life as I grew to love him as my own family, as opposed to being thought of as my stepdad, and also referred to him as dad.

We set up our new home on August 25th the year of 1972, in Staveley, close to Chesterfield, not a million miles away and our house was a beautiful mobile home on a caravan site. We'd purchased it from Newark Caravans and had it delivered to the site. This seemed a fun novelty as a kid at first and we went onto having a fun-filled year in this place as a new family. My real dad was very much on the scene for me too and regular weekends he would come over to our home and pick me up. I really looked forward to seeing him, as I'd gone from him being around every day, doing every day stuff for four years, to becoming my dad I saw only at weekends. We'd have the same fun we had before my parents split, and it was great to spend time with Sharon and David again. I missed them too. We'd go on outings together or spend time at home, I loved them all so much. When it came to the end of the weekends with my dad, it troubled me, and I would feel the tears pricking which always led onto a full-blown, inconsolable crying bout. In my mind, I felt very sad to be saying goodbye to my dad, but also felt heartbroken and worried about wanting to be with my mum and other dad. I was acutely aware of not wanting to upset any of them. It was a torrent of emotions that felt quite a lot to deal with at first. Apart from these times of being handed over from my dad to my mum, I kept my thoughts to myself mostly and learned to cope with my feelings. I spent most of the time feeling happy and was lavished with attention but it was tinged with a little sadness at the situation. It's amazing just how resilient children are, before they have been conditioned with what society dictates to them on how to feel, how to behave and suchlike.

My big childhood dream was to become a musician - I absolutely loved making music, or trying to as the case may be. Although mum and dad did not have lots of money back then, they got me everything that they could afford and the Christmas of 1972 saw me excitedly tearing into a gift wrapped set of drums. My first proper instrument and how I delighted in testing those out - in the caravan! The loud bangs and crashes of the cymbals echoed throughout the shell of the van with encouragement from my parents to perform, everything revolved around little me. I was perhaps a little spoilt with attention and it was probably them, in their own way, trying to make up for the split. My sheer delight would fast turn to frustrated tantrums, when I realised I wasn't able to play tunefully straight away and would take to storming off in a mardy moment. Over the childhood years I went through a stream of different musical instruments, such as guitars, organs and others, and I never learned to play a single one of them, not to sound half decent anyway, probably to the dismay of my parent's eardrums.

Twelve months later, we moved home again, to Oak Avenue, in Farndon as my parents were awarded a council house. Mum married my stepdad and life was idyllic. I was confused to why my mum had changed her name to "Knight." I was extremely conscious of it and the thought of changing my name upset me as it may upset my dad, which my little heart could not bear. I was the only child at school with a different name to my dad (Fred) and they'd question me about it on school trips when full names were used. It was hard and made me feel very different. I had no issues at all with my mum and my stepdad Fred but demonstrates the empathy of a young child. Looking back, I wish I had changed my name to match my mum's new name. Fred's daughter, Therese, who I spent time with as a child, has no contact with him now.

My parents were hardworking folk; mum was the canteen manager of a large textile factory, whilst my dad, worked for an engineering firm. This house backed onto the rear of a field, an absolute dream for a kid. If you gave me a football to play, I was as happy as can be. Weekend's would start early, around 7am, because as soon as I was awake, I'd be rushing to get out of the front door and play. The neighbourhood's kids would congregate on this field and it was one almighty playground for us, such great fun. The days would pass kicking a ball around the field, playing in the adjoined woods and generally enjoying those exciting childhood adventures with my buddies. I'd return home when I was hungry, then race straight back outside to play all over again, only going back home when the skies started to darken.

Time gone by, those were the days.

2
Mischievous Me

I was described as a bit of a mischievous character, full of adventure and fun, which led me to experience numerous scrapes over the years. When I was attending pre-school, I was a good boy but had this slightly wilder, daring streak. Our garden had a fence that separated it from a river that ran along the bottom of the garden. One day, my parents heard me shouting loudly for help. When they rushed outside to my rescue, to their joint amusement and shock, they discovered me hanging precariously by my cobalt blue jumper which had got lodged onto a nail protruding out of the five foot high wooden fence. The scary part was - that if they had not heard me and found me at that moment, I may possibly have drowned in the cold waters below, as I was not a swimmer at that age.

Then there was the day that it had seemed a good idea to paint with my friend, a neighbour's little girl. It wasn't on paper though, as that seemed dull, but my dad's garage took a generous coating of a bright shade of apple green. We didn't stop there either as it seemed a lot more fun to cover ourselves from head to toe in the gloopy emulsion too, we looked a comical pair as we matched up to the garage's interior. My parents were not quite as pleased with the finished result however. I think my artistic streak was brought into life this day.

I wore hats everywhere, I was mad about them. If we went anywhere, the first thing we were guaranteed to do was to make a hat stop. To buy me another. Most kids hated having to wear any form of headwear, but not me, I was in my element. I loved to be different, and in my heart, being different was something I yearned for, having no desire to blend in with the crowds of other kids. I'd wear them inside the house too, whilst bashing tunes out of my favourite musical instrument of the moment.

Life was grand, the stuff happy childhoods are made of. We were just an ordinary working-class family, with very few materialistic possessions to speak of, but oodles of love, fun and laughter filled our merry household daily. I adapted well to my parents living apart, still maintaining a good relationship with my real dad. I loved my stepdad, whom I will keep referring to as dad, we were all very close and I felt very cared for. Maybe this was why I felt I dared to do some of the escapades I found myself involved in, because I felt accepted for who I was. No-one was going to judge me or tell me I was stupid. It was safe.

My friends were an important part of my life too and they, themselves, felt like an extended family. Sean Toon, Jason Jones, Lee Payne (and I best mention Dean Sugden), were amongst my best mates and we shared some fantastic times.

Picking a vibrant bunch of daffodils from my neighbour's garden seemed a lovely thing to do, I gave them to my mum as a present as I wanted to make her smile. It didn't strike me as wrong or naughty at the time. Nor the occasion that I ran off from home with my friend, on a new adventure. We wound up in a builder's hut of all places, and in a moment of worry, not knowing our way home, we scribbled a note with a dusty, chewed up pen we came across and left it out for the postman to find. The time passed by and as it began to get dusky, we both drifted into a slumber after the day's excitement. Meanwhile, some of the neighbourhood, friends and the police were searching for us and found us curled up in two corners of the hut, covered in dust.

My passion for all things musical continued as I got older, and each holiday we had, my mum and dad would take me to the theatre to see the shows. I'd be beyond excited, but not long after the lights dimmed for the performance to begin, I'd have fallen asleep. Mum suggested they try the matinee shows to avoid my sleepiness, but the same behaviour was repeated. I seemed to associate the darkness with my bedtime habit. One of my many instrumental experiments was an electric guitar. Of course, I initially had no idea how to make the gadget make beautiful music so my parents found a local tutor to give me lessons. After a short time however, the instructor informed my mum that he would no longer be giving me further lessons. Apparently, I had bigger ideas, and declared, much to his tested patience, that I wanted to become an overnight popstar. It wasn't long, before the novelty had worn off and the electric guitar was gathering dust amongst the pile of other redundant instruments. And there were no signs of a budding pop sensation about to make his debut either.

3
The Broadway, CB Radios and A Packet Of Crisps

Schooldays had been fun years so far, my happy childhood spilling into the time spent sitting behind the wooden desks. I was known as the class clown and loved nothing more than making others laugh, the jokey entertainer in me thrived on this. I was still seeing my real dad, and truthfully, a part of my jokey exterior was to hide the insecurities that I felt. It was my own self-produced coping mechanism. Seven years down the line, I still felt that a part of me could not be perceived as being too happy seeing my dad as that may upset my mum and other dad. It felt natural for me to take on this protective role to prevent the people that I loved most in this world from getting hurt. In fact, I always did this for everyone. My heart knew that what you say, the words you use, and how you say it, will affect others. I did not recognise this as empathy as a ten year old lad.

We were still living in the square of council houses, adjacent to the fields. I was friends with everyone and was never involved in any fights like some of the lads, even the bullies I made friends out of. It had such a strong sense of community and all looking out for one another. After school, I would spend a lot of time with my aunty Ivy as my mum would be working, I had fun times with my aunty too as my cousin Sarah was the same age as me and we became very close friends spending so much time together after school. Mum would collect me each day once she'd finished her shift in the canteen, it was a hard and manual job, then we'd go home and she'd busy herself in the kitchen once more, preparing my dad's tea. No-one had very much money at the time, but it was certainly made up for with love. We had nothing, but we had everything.

During the last year at my primary school, when I was ten, Mrs. Meldrum was one of my teachers, I was very fond of her and we were her first class that she had taught. There was a slight sense of competition as we were all vying for Mrs. Meldrum's attention and wanted to be her favourite. She was a popular lady.

My parents decided on pursuing a different lifestyle by going into the license trade. Apparently, my dad had always had a hankering to run a pub. After some research, a public house called *The Broadway Hotel* became available for them to take over. This required us to all move area as the pub was located in Newark. It created a certain amount of apprehension for me at this time as it would mean leaving my set of friends that I'd grown up with and gone through the years at primary with, plus the friends of different ages to me in my neighbourhood. It was an especially big deal for a ten year old as I would be in a different catchment for my schooling, which meant changing to a new school. Then there was the disruption to my school work, I was not too pleased at all of the changes before me.

To most people, I was seen as an outgoing character. This was true, except when I was with people that I didn't know. Then my self-confidence would take a dip and my inner shyness would show itself. I only knew one person at the new school, which I found a challenge to start with in the initial weeks of the changeover. The school seemed to consider these matters and noted my sensitivity as they placed me in the same class as the lad that I already knew. This surely helped me to adjust. It was only a matter of time, a few weeks, before I had settled in and made lots of new friends. At this time in my life, it seemed that if I experienced a bit of a knock whilst I was going forwards, I'd pull myself back a little but it wouldn't be long before I bounced back.

Living at the pub was a very different way of life altogether, for all of us. I experienced a new level of freedom, which for the young lad heading into puberty that I was, it proved to be a bittersweet time. The positive being the time I had alone in the evenings, to watch what I wanted on television, to do what I felt like doing generally. It was great actually, with no parent breathing down my neck to get homework done or to do this or that chore. I felt like a mini version of the adult Jason in charge of his kingdom. A big bonus was the pub being so large. Downstairs was the bar, lounge and kitchen areas that I didn't spend as much time in, but upstairs was a different story. Five spacious bedrooms occupied the floor plus the bathrooms. Mum and dad took up just one of those rooms and the remainder were free, and I regularly changed which bedroom I slept in. I was spoilt for choice and each room had a different feel to it for me, it was a bit like having the novelty of being on vacation but not actually going anywhere. Plus an abundance of space to spread my belongings, including my prized instruments and footballs in. Posters adorned the bedroom walls of my favourite football players and when my new friends came over sometimes, they were amazed at my having all of this space I called my own. Of course, there was also the "crême de la crême" of having parents that owned a pub - the unlimited supply of crisps and pop. As I ventured into my teens, the pop was occasionally replaced by sneaky bottles of cider or lager. One of my little jobs was to do the bottling up, and if there was ever a party I was going to, the odd bottle would go astray and I'd pop the money in the till. My best friend at the time, was my faithful companion, Zeb. A striking golden retriever with a glossy coat. We spent many evenings in front of the television, drawing - I loved my art projects or messing around in one of my bedrooms. He was good company, as the downside of parents running a pub, as I discovered, was that the evenings could stretch out to be rather lonely as the months went by. It was through this loneliness that I got interested in CB Radios. They were all the rage at the time but really helped me to not feel as isolated, providing me with that all-important human connection. I made lots of friends through the airwaves and each of us had our own radio names and some code to talk in. It was a great source of amusement for me, especially throughout the dark winter months.

The Broadway Hotel was a large and bustling pub, one of two serving our estate. There would be entertainment each weekend, with vocalists and other entertainers bringing in the crowds. My mum loved nothing more than to get involved in the singing, especially after she had enjoyed a few tipples herself. I would hear her belting out her favourite tunes and the pub crowd cheering the landlady on. The place had much character, mainly down to my parent's passion for what they put into running the pub and also the collection of customers that came through the doors. Characters from all walks of life, all working class with many erring towards a rough and ready outlook. Some of these customers would do anything to get by, as times were tough financially. There were some tales told within those four walls, especially when they were fuelled by alcohol. My parents were actually more financially better off at this stage but they had barely any free time to spend it and enjoy it, due to the demands of the working lifestyle. Each day, I was allowed to play pool downstairs with my dad at 5pm and I looked forward to this hour so much, our special time. Then at 6pm the doors were opened to the public. We'd see our loyal regulars every day and I could stay downstairs to play a couple of more games of pool with those folks too that came for early doors. I enjoyed the friendly banter we'd have and the atmosphere of being a part of a close community. We were one big family. Like clockwork, my mum would be serving behind the bar by 8pm each evening as the pub filled up, this is when I'd be upstairs entertaining myself.

One weekend I was hanging around with some of my mates from the estate, we were just milling about and found ourselves near to the old dilapidated part of the brewery. It had smashed in windows and had been derelict for ages so it seemed harmless to go inside. It was great fun as we climbed up to the old beams 30ft in the air, what an adventure for a Sunday afternoon. We had a blast. Just as we were leaving the dusty old shell of a building we spotted a storeroom opposite the exit. Curiosity getting the better of us, we peered inside and saw crates and crates of beer. It must have been really old as you could tell it had all been opened and the smell of stale ale lingered in the dank room.

The temptation was too much and we each grabbed a couple of bottles and fled outside. We scrambled over the brick wall outside and plonked ourselves down on the other side, clinking the bottles as we went. We guzzled the beer, all making out it tasted nice when in fact it was a little stale. We soon got tiddly as we laughed our heads off at our antics. The next moment, two faces peered over the wall and we spotted the tell-tale helmets. The police. They proceeded to arrest all of us as they assumed we were responsible to the damage caused to the brewery. We'd smashed a few glass panes but it was wrecked prior to our arrival. They carted us off to the police station, I was alarmed and worried what my mum and dad would say. What would I tell them? I had to spend a couple of hours in a police cell and when I was questioned, I spilled the beans on everything. Luckily for us, dad worked for that brewery with the pub and was able to smooth things over, but I'll never forget being driven home in a police car. It was me, Jason, trying to fit in with the crowd again and not speaking up when I knew it wasn't the right thing to do. I just went along with it and had to suffer the consequences.

Now settled back into school life, I was performing well. Mum praised me as I was in all of the top sets at school, I loved the sense of achievement it brought me. In hindsight, I could have tried harder and accomplished more as I still played out the role of class clown somewhat. I got a buzz from making my friends laugh, and the more they encouraged it, the more I obliged. I realise now, that it was masking the insecurities that I felt deep down, as I was not naturally all that confident. Aspiring to be different and seen as different never left me either. Again, I think this was a cover up as to how I really felt within. An obvious way of standing out was through your appearance and I embraced the whole mod scene of that era. My brother, David, was a massive influence on me and I admired him so much and longed to be more like him. On his visits to see us, he always travelled on his scooter and he worshipped the Northern Soul music scene. I would lap up his stories that he shared with me and his tales of Northern Soul all-nighters. I would excitedly sit on his scooter, feeling the epitome of my own version of mod, with my always, smart appearance, my iconic green fishtail parka and my hair coiffured into a spiky style. A very fashion conscious young lad I was and was passionate about the mod music scene also, it was everything. The Jam were my idols, next to David, and I loved sharing my music interest with him.

My shyness kept me at a distance with the opposite sex, even though I had a healthy interest as a hormonal teenage boy. I hung around in a gang, mostly other mods and there was one girl that I had a secret crush on. She was the best looking girl in the gang, really pretty. We were really good friends and shared one kiss. That's all it was, but I never forgot it and even remembered it years later. All of the intense emotions, such was teenage life.

4
The End of an Era

Six years of pub life was taking its toll on my parent's relationship. The long relentless hours of this type of demanding work and living in your workspace blurred into a version of all work, and no play. Eventually my mum issued my dad an ultimatum - they either gave it all up or their marriage was over. It had worn her down and she recognised the impact before my dad had, but you could see the strain on them both. It was great whilst it had lasted but the good times were over.

It was at a crucial time in my education as it was the year before my main exams that would predict my future. None of us had anywhere to live, as once you gave up the business, your accommodation was gone with it. Also requiring work, my mum went to work and live at my aunty's pub in Dinnington, Sheffield. It was called *The Cutler*. My dad found employment as a steel erector which needed him to work away for a short time. It gave my parents breathing space too and time to adjust to their new paths. I, however, was not keen to go anywhere, as I was settled with my friends and more importantly, at school. Arrangements were made for me to live with my sister so that I could maintain the focus on my work and forthcoming exams with the least amount of disruption as possible.

Three months later, my parents had settled but I had become very unsettled. I'd somehow lost my mojo towards my academic work and was neglecting both my homework and my attendance to lessons. My work went downhill considerably and I began to get poor results. It was frustrating, but I became even more focussed on my artwork, I loved nothing more than to copy draw and paint. Recreating music albums was my favourite pastime and I'd get lost in my creativity. The quality of my art never deteriorated and if anything, improved with the extra attention it was given.

The decision for me to move to Sheffield to join my parents was made, with the aim of me refocussing on my schoolwork and to undo the damage that had occurred. At the same time, my mum came out of my aunt's pub, my dad came home from his away job, both finding new work and they reconciled their relationship properly. It was not as easy for me to make amends with my situation and my quality of work never recovered to where it was before. It was tough being in the final year of a new school, having to make friends all over again whilst my exams were looming. I felt pressured. I tried frantically to fit in, not wanting to be the new, shy student yet again. It seemed harder at fifteen than six years previously, as myself and my peers were all more aware of anything or anyone being different. I was lucky in that my older cousin, Tim, was there and he took me under his wing.

Tim was popular and everyone seemed to know him in that area which benefitted me as it brought me his friendship groups to associate with, he was an influence on me that I was very grateful for at the time. They were all older than me and seemed quite more mature, I felt the difference, but this prevented anyone from singling me out and picking on me. There was always a silver lining in every darker cloud I found, whatever the situation was. Hanging around in an older crowd, meant that I was doing older activities, including nights out at local nightclubs and drinking more than ever before. There was rarely any difficulty in my being admitted by the doormen, as I blended in with the other guys. As they were older, most of them were driving and had cars, this was a great perk of having older mates. I used to get ferried around in the boot of one of their cars, it was such a laugh.

Most of the time I was at home, I'd be engaged in my art, I always had a pencil or paint in my hand ready to recreate some object. It was escapism for me and I excelled in my passion. It was just as well really, as my schoolwork still suffered, but all I truly wanted to pursue was to use my copy-artist skills in a job. My previous ambitions of becoming a pop star had long diminished, art was my future.

My aunty gave me a part time job in her pub to earn myself some pocket money doing odd jobs, like collecting glasses and emptying ash trays, but she actually paid me very generously and I was able to spend my wages and save some which enabled me to join in ventures with the older crowd who were all working themselves.

The day I received the news of my exam results, I was in Majorca, holidaying with the lads. As predicted, they were not great, but I was over the moon as all I cared about was having the basics such as English, Maths and of course Art in order to follow my art dreams. My mum and dad were disappointed as they had thoughts of me going to university but I knew what I was destined for, I was a creative and needed to use my natural ability.

During my sixteenth year, we moved home again. Back to the familiar territory of Farndon and its fond childhood memories. At first, we had no choice but to live with my sister, which was a little cramped but then my parents managed to get a council house on California Road. My school years were over and it was time to become an adult, which meant I had to find work. In those days, YTS schemes were the popular option for school leavers, it gave a young person the opportunity to learn a trade whilst earning a small wage. I ended up in a garage for six months, as there was not a lot else available. I hated it from the word go, as mechanics was probably as far removed from where my heart lay as possible. I was not a practical, getting hands dirty kind of lad, and longed to be doing something with my creativity. I did enjoy having a wage though and the lifestyle I could enjoy with that with my mates. Earning £25 a week, my mum would take £5 off of me to contribute towards my board, then I saved a little and splurged the rest on fun times. Over time, my mum was quietly putting aside my board money and once it had mounted up she was able to furnish our home with a new carpet, such a luxury. I always joked with her for a long time afterwards, about how I'd bought that carpet!

During a conversation with David, my brother, one weekend when he came to visit us, he could tell how much I disliked what I was doing at the garage. I shared with him that what I really wanted to do was to become a sign writer and use my skills and express my artistic flair. He suggested that I research companies in the Yellow Pages directory and apply to the relevant firms that provided sign writing services.

What a great idea! His words were, "if you want it, go out and get it." This inspired me a lot to do exactly that and he went even further up in my estimation that day as my role model to aspire towards.

Within a short space of time, and several work applications later, I was excited to receive an offer of an interview at a Newark company of sign writers in January 1985. It would be a dream come true to work there and I enthusiastically prepared myself for the appointment. They requested to see some samples of my work at the interview, and were so impressed with my ability that they immediately employed me as an apprentice even though they already had one young guy on their books. It was a thrilling bonus to find out that on top of my regular YTS scheme payment they added an additional £7.50 on the top. As a sixteen year old, I felt like a millionaire! My mum increased my board accordingly. I felt elated and proud of myself for achieving this opportunity to learn and prosper in my dream career. The firm manufactured replica 1920's vehicles that required a specialist sign writing, and these were shipped all around the world. It was a steep learning curve which required me to practice, practice and practice some more. I started at the bottom with all of the little jobs and once I'd mastered these, I'd be moved onto the next stage. It was a highly skilled profession and I was privileged to be learning from John Cooper, who was a nationally recognised sign writer, he made a great boss too and I loved my job. Learning on the job continually, I gradually got better and better, resulting in a career at which I had become brilliant at my craft.

Passing my driving test was a great moment, as for every teenager, it's a big milestone and you instantly feel more grown up. Whilst my dad was working away at times, I was allowed to use the family car. My dad was not so impressed when he came home at weekends to find a dirty vehicle and the petrol tank heavily drained from my usage. Of course, I had to go and have another first milestone by way of a bump. Purely an accident, but I ran into the rear of another car causing damage to his bumper. He only turned out to be a vicar of all people. The repairs set me back around £90 and some odd pence which was a lot for me in those days, three weeks wages to be precise. I was fuming when I went to see the vicar to pay for the repair, as before I'd even had chance to reach into my pocket for my wallet, he swiftly reminded me of the pence that I also owed him. I remember feeling a sense of shock as he had not only given me a chance to pay before jumping down my throat but he was a vicar, where was the compassion?

When I wasn't working, you would either find me playing or watching football, my second passion, or socialising with my circle of friends. Football was a huge part of my life all of my teens, right from playing in the school team. Then I was in the local team, Farndon Football Club and an avid supporter of Nottingham Forest. I loved going to as many of their matches, home and away, with my friends as possible. Part of the passion for me was the camaraderie that goes with the sport, I had some great friendships that meant a lot to me. This was the total sum of my life at that time.

I used to hang around with Lee Payne a lot at this time, we would go down the local spending all our money on beer and on nights when we were skint, we would sit around his mum and dad's while they were out. They always had a good selection of alcohol and we would help ourselves to a few shots of his dad's vodka.

All of my mates were coupled up and I felt the odd one out without a girlfriend but I was always busy with my two main interests. It was on a Saturday night at the local *Rose and Crown* pub in Farndon, that I met Paula. She was a pretty girl. We were in the same social circle and our families knew each other. Strangely enough, we had nothing in common whatsoever, but we somehow found ourselves going out together. They say that opposites attract, but I think you can be too different. She hated football and couldn't stand the sight of most of my friends, not exactly a match made in heaven. We had a rather volatile relationship that was as much off as it was on and the term "boyfriend and girlfriend" was very loosely used. This continued in this fashion for the next two years, if we split up, as we frequently did, we'd be reunited again by the following Friday night in the pub. We'd while away the weekends in the pub, drinking, with the football interludes and then Saturday nights we would all go into the town to the nightclub. Young, free and half single.

5
Bittersweet Memories

Although I got on okay with Paula's family, I knew her sister, Lisa, best of all as we were at school together being the same age. Our relationship felt the strain further and further. We bickered a lot of the time, it was like we were the opposite bookends with the long distance apart, just about hanging in there. It's as though we ended up together out of convenience and to be with 'someone' as everyone else in the gang were.

I kept my love for football as it kept me going and each Saturday I would be off with my friends to see the latest match. In my heart, I knew that this relationship did not have the basis for any longevity and could not visualise a future with Paula. Admitting that to myself secretly pricked some feelings of guilt, but I could tell that the feeling was mutual. As fast as the thought sprung into my mind, I buried it again and just got on with things.

It was a huge shock when Paula announced that she was pregnant. It came completely out of the blue and was definitely not part of our plan. I can remember the rise in her voice as she told me followed by a long pause. As I clutched at my throat, and struggled to find my voice initially, I couldn't help the disbelieving tone that I heard coming from myself as I uttered some questioning words to help me clarify and comprehend this new information that had been thrust upon me. I felt my heart racing as though it was attempting to pound furiously enough to escape my chest, my mind in a whirl of fuzzy thoughts. I sensed her apprehension as she awaited my reaction, her muscles tightened and her whole body clenching tightly. After what felt like an age, I blurted something and grabbed her in a mix of shock, fear, anger and happiness, my emotions were all over the place as it sunk it the seriousness of this moment and the huge impact that this news was going to make to both of our lives.

Our news, once processed, and the initial shock released, brought feelings of hope for our relationship and future happiness, as well as concerns about the sober responsibility of being a parent, how on earth we were financially going to cope and probably the scariest aspect, telling my parents. I was terrified of what they would say and think. Each time the thought came into my mind, I felt a tremble start within me and my skin would start to feel a very uncomfortable clamminess. In the end, Paula did the deed. My beloved team, Nottingham Forest were playing away at Norwich and I went to the match and it just so happened that my dad was also away. Paula used this opportunity to call round to see my mum and share the news. Then my mum told my dad. I know they had mixed reservations as they knew we were not all that well matched. However, we were inclined to stay together, it wasn't just about us anymore, we had a baby to consider, another little person's life.

From then onwards, everything changed. My wages had to be saved up towards a home for us and that was just the first sacrifice. We took the plunge to live together, as in just a few months' time we would be a family. Paula moved into my parent's house, but the strain of all living together under one roof was too much so we packed up and moved in with Paula's family instead. It helped us to save as well and all of my earnings were spoken for, and our socialising was reduced as we had a tight budget to adjust to. By the time our baby daughter was born on March 16th 1990, we had everything we needed to provide for becoming a family.

It had been a drawn out labour before she was born safely in hospital. I felt an instant surge of deep love as I cast eyes on our daughter and held her for the first time. We named our beautiful little girl, Abbi. The feelings of elation were like nothing I had ever felt before and the pride at becoming a daddy. I doted on Abbi and her with me, and we formed a very close loving bond from day one, more so than with her mum.

Watching Abbi grow and change over the next few months was incredible, the milestones that every proud parent witnesses. Neither Paula nor I were truthfully happy still, but I was determined to make this work for Abbi's sake. A few months later, we managed to get a council house in Farndon and it was a relief to have our own space. Paula was a stay at home mum. My parents had been very house proud. Each day at home, I had to make my bed, keeping my room tidy and mow the lawn whilst my dad was working away. Mum always remarked on what a good job I did! My wife wasn't that interested in keeping a tidy home though. It was tough and we were just keeping our heads above water. We still wanted to go out at weekends as we were very young, and we scraped through.

We drifted into a decision to get married, again for the sake of providing a solid family unit for Abbi and what was expected of us by society and family. To help ease our financial burdens, I got some sign writing work at the weekends, painting people's vans for their businesses. It struck me though that money really doesn't bring happiness as I noted the comparison of my parents having nothing when I was younger but of how happy they were as opposed to us. We got married at Farndon church on October 13th 1990, funded by both our sets of parents. It was a big gathering with the usual bridesmaids, guys in tails, Paula dressed in white. The shining star of the show was Abbi. Dressed up as a beautiful little bridesmaid and was still young as to be carried down the aisle and held throughout the day. It was followed by a nice reception at the *Robin Hood Hotel* in Newark. Everybody in our community held their reception there and we had a knee's up. Deep down, my heart wasn't in it but felt the pressure to conform. We didn't have a honeymoon.

On April 12th 1991, Nottingham Forest got to Wembley in a momentous occasion. What should have been the celebration of a lifetime ended up being massively crushing disappointment. I'd had to borrow money for my ticket originally, but then after losing my beloved job, I just could not afford to go. I was forced into selling my ticket for £100. I could not believe that I had to miss out on the final, especially as all of my friends were there. I never quite recovered from missing out on this, it really felt like the nail in the coffin.

We soldiered on, more cracks appearing in our relationship. I didn't feel that happy but kept everything to myself and focussed on my work and on bringing up Abbi. The recession hit our country which affected my job meaning reduced hours and less pay. They got rid of some of the staff which piled on the pressure at home. We rowed even more and we both felt really miserable. It was awful. The stress drove Paula and I to drink more at weekends, getting blind drunk every weekend, I felt as though my work was stringing me along and I knew I was clinging onto the hours I had left for dear life. We really wanted to make it work however, and it seemed a good idea to try for another baby, and sure enough, Paula fell pregnant for the second time in the October time.

By the February of 1992, things at work worsened and I was delivered the shattering news of redundancy. I knew it had only been a matter of time. Times were very tough and it all seemed so bleak. I felt my mind-set darken as my self-esteem took a real knock with my dream job ending too. Why was this happening to us? It seemed like one bad thing after another. As well as the financial pressure, and our relationship feeling dead, I had to sacrifice another love of mine - I had to give up my football altogether. The resentment of being with Paula multiplied, we should not be together, yet I had made my decision so I had to live with it.

The only good thing in my life at that time was my daughter. Abbi developed her own little character and had spirit at that young age along with her warm, loving nature. I still went to play football in our local team on a Sunday morning, and when I came back and was having a soak in the bath, I could sense that she'd be outside the bathroom door, not wanting to leave my side. When she woke up during the night, it would be me that she wanted, instead of her mum.

It was more unusual than with a lot of children. I knew how much I wanted to make her feel secure and loved as I recalled the insecurities I felt as I grew up with my parents splitting up and when my dad worked away. I did not want my little princess to ever feel this as I felt that fierce protectiveness towards her. I could see elements of her mum in her, but she was more influenced by me with the bond we had and it showed.

May of 1992 was the birth of our son, Samuel. How lovely to have one of each sex. Samuel was a good baby, and for a while, everything felt fantastic again. We were papering over the cracks really but we did think that another baby would solve our problems and bring us closer together. Money was a burning issue again for us as I'd been out of work for a while and now we had two babies to provide for. I was relieved to find some temporary work through a friend. It was seasonal throughout the summer months, and whilst needs must and it paid our bills, I hated working at the power stations, even though the short contract work paid very generously. They were long shifts and I was working seven days a week. As soon as I'd got home after a shift, I saw my children, had something to eat, I had to sleep to be ready for the next working day. I didn't get to spend as much time with Sam as a baby which saddened me but times were tougher than ever.

It was exhausting, but I knew part of the tiredness was down to the ongoing stress I felt under. The work was at two local sites when I first began. I was not spending much time with my family at all and it was the toughest time yet. When we did go out at the weekend, it would be separately, me on a Friday night and Paula on the Saturday, or vice versa whilst the other one stayed at home to babysit. I was still having to get up early the following morning for work and Paula with the children. I felt as though I had to grow up very quickly during this year. The next contract at work resulted us into working away from home for a month. The strain showed as we completely grew apart. By the October, I was laid off as the contract came to an end. With no job, no prospects and no money, it hit us hard. We were young and so when we had experienced some money in our pockets again, we had spent it and not saved anything. The only blessing was that I could at last spend much more time with Sam and Abbi.

6
Trauma

Those autumnal weeks dragged by, it was turning into a cold season as the leaves added touches of colour to the otherwise dark and gloomy atmosphere. My own mood was turning gloomier by the day also, as not working and the dismal situation at home was really getting to me by this point.

I should have been looking forward to a family Christmas and Samuel's first one, but our financial state was desperate and we were only just scraping by to pay the bills. It worried me sick, I kept it to myself as much as I could, but it spilled out in moments of feeling more emotional and was a trigger to many rows between my wife and I. It made me feel rubbish as the supposed breadwinner that I wasn't providing for my family, my self-worth was at an all-time low.

At the start of December some work came my way, thankfully. Whilst grateful for the opportunity to earn some money from Paula's dad whom ran a roofing company, I absolutely detested the work itself. It meant working outside in the bitter cold on a building site, low morale - a far cry from the sign writing work that I loved to do. Needs must for my family and I reminded myself it was just a short term solution to get us through the Christmas festivities and the financial demands that brought with it.

Christmas itself was abysmal. I felt so guilty and ashamed of myself as we could not even afford to buy Christmas cards for our family and friends, never mind presents. It was the first time ever and I vowed that it would never happen again. We scraped enough together somehow to buy some toys for the kids so they had something to unwrap and get excited about from Santa. On Christmas Day itself, my family invited us to go to spend the day with them. Mum and Dad were really sympathetic and understanding but I just remember the sick feeling in my stomach of humiliation. Other members of our family were there but I couldn't face seeing them to start with and sat on the stairs in the hall refusing to go into the living room with the rest of the crowd. As I sat there on the hard step, feeling the chill around my legs and hearing the sounds of joviality from the other side of the door, I felt tears pricking and inside I felt as though my world was collapsing before me. I pulled myself together as my little nephew came out to me and sat on the stairs for a while with me, it touched me but I felt very silly at the same time, as though I was the child. After a while, and some coaxing, I reluctantly went into the lounge area to join the rest of the family. I made some lame excuses not to be involved in their merry making, trying my hardest to use my fail safe tactic of humour, but even that had waned. I sat on the side lines all day until it was time to go home, watching distantly at the pulling of crackers around the dinner table, silly jokes, the kids playing with their new toys, the incessant chatter of the adults and the faint drone of Christmas carols in the background. I wasn't sure how I got through that day, it was so hard, as it struck me just how much I had changed. I'd gone from being a very happy go lucky person to this. The series of events and the run of bad luck and choice to stay with my wife had ground me down. As the saying goes - I had made my bed so I must lie in it.

The week between Christmas and New Year dragged. I drank quite heavily at times to cope with how I felt all the time, feeling shame and guilt that I should be a happy dad and husband, not the failure that I had become. I was trying to drum up thoughts of New Year, new start and all of that positive malarkey but it didn't quite feel true. Whilst I wanted to make resolutions and fresh plans the low mood persisted. I did resolve to remain committed as I did not want my marriage to fail for the sake of our kids. I had prominent memories of what that felt like for me as a child, the insecurity I felt at that time and I did not want my kids to feel that pain. I had to put my own happiness to one side, buckle up and get on with it, there was no other alternative as far as I was concerned.

New Year's Eve came round, the kids had played non-stop with their new toys all week, they were such good children. Paula's aunty had offered to baby sit that evening so that Paula and I could go a party at the pub. We got dressed up for the night ahead, I made a bit of an effort, it was New Year's Eve after all, the most celebrated night of the year down at the pub. Paula didn't like a lot of people, especially my mates and their partners, for no reason. She especially hated one of my close friend's girlfriend. She seemed jealous of her, you could see the vicious glare in her eyes. Later on in the evening, after drinking a fair amount along with everyone else and feeling merry, I got up to dance with another woman. It was the woman that Paula hated with a passion. For the first time ever in my marriage, I felt a spark on that dance floor, that felt like it was more than just a dance. I don't know if the woman felt it too, but as good as it felt, I brushed it aside as I reminded myself that she was married to my mate and that I had my wife. I felt mixed emotions of half wanting it to be over but of it to not end at the same time as I was enjoying the moment. Maybe part of that was because I knew it would provoke a reaction from Paula, I wanted her to react, as even though we had to remain married for the kid's sake, I really did not want to be with her. Talk about conflicted feelings.

On January 2nd 1993, we were partying again. This time it was someone's 21st, from our gang. There were all of the familiar friendly faces gather in the local again, a feeling of dĕja vu set in, it was as though we'd been there since New Year's Eve. Another familiarity was that the girl I'd danced with just two nights before, was also there again. A thought that crossed my mind was that I needed to test the waters to see if there was anything between us, some kind of attraction and if it was mutual. At the same time, thoughts flashed into my head of Paula and how distant we had become and the long term tension and emptiness there now was. I could not help to feel some satisfaction from winding her up by showing this other female some attention, as another thought I had was a suspicion that Paula was actually having an affair behind my back. This really angered me obviously, and added fuel to the fire. The weeks that I had been working away in recent months and all of the Friday and Saturday nights we had ventured out separately and her not returning home at the end of a night out. I'd had a growing niggle that something was amiss. When you know a person well, inside out, you can feel it without any stark factual evidence. Call it gut instinct. It was like a huge rift that I had no idea how to come back from. Then, when my kids popped into my head, I felt overwhelming guilt and pushed all thoughts of this other woman out of my head. How dumb was I being? It turned into yet another evening of heavy drinking, trying to mask how I was truly feeling by joining in as much as I felt I could with the jolly behaviour of our friendship group.

Boy, did I have a hangover the following morning. We'd stayed out drinking until about 3.30am, which was heavy going by my standards. I had no intention of working that day, January 3rd. I knew the night before, as the party got into full swing, that I'd be spending the next day nursing the hangover from hell whilst spending precious time with the kids and also trying to figure out my future. I was still in bed, when there was a loud knock on our front door. I groaned as I answered the door with bleary eyes and a pounding head. As I opened the door, the cold January air hit me and I shivered in my stripy pyjamas, I must have looked rough as Kenny looked me up and down as though I'd been dragged through a hedge or something.

"Are you coming out to work today or what Jase?"

After another inward groan, I dashed back into the warmth of my house and grabbed my stuff together and threw on some clothes. It was going to be freezing working outside that day, so I piled on the layers. Jeans, t-shirt, sweatshirt, my favourite Adidas hoody, trainers and an insulated jacket. I needed the income and if I showed willing, it may lead to further work, as much as I hated it.

In the car, we had some banter, there was Paula's dad, Keith driving. We joked about the drunken antics of the night before, but they had both been a lot more sensible by leaving at a reasonable time. Not me, I'd really gone for it in the depressive slumber I was living in. It grieved me as well to think that yet again, I was missing out on a crucial match that Nottingham Forest were playing. I should have been there, happy with my mates, rather than freezing my ass of in a job I hated with a passion.

We headed to our site for the day, it was a relief to find out it was a flat roof job, these were much safer to be spending time on. I spent the morning trying to do as little as possible, still feeling the effects of the alcohol from the previous night. My head felt foggy and I was tired. The headache slowly decreased over the morning and the crisp cold air certainly helped. I confided in Kenny a little, as both he and Keith, knew that Paula and I were having problems. I couldn't really speak to Keith about it with him being her dad, that felt too weird. It helped to talk, it relieved the pain a little briefly but I still felt fed up and hugely frustrated.

Towards the end of the shift, I had sobered up much more but was feeling the effects of being outside all day, the temperature must have been freezing, or it certainly seemed it. Keith received a call asking to go onto another job. Part of me just wanted to get home to the warmth but the other part of me knew I should do it for the money and the chance of more opportunities. So I agreed.

It was an old RAF building, located in-between Newark and Nottingham, so right out in the countryside. It had been converted into an Islamic school and they needed repairs doing to the roof. On their request, we followed through with their instructions without really challenging them. We were aware that their health and safety laws were not the same as the UK regulations, and as it was a cash in hand job, it was easier to just get on with it.

It was even chillier now and I was relieved that it was only a quick job. With the two of us working on it, the job should be done within the hour. I held the ladder and weighted it for Keith as he went onto the roof first, and I followed. I knew it was not right, taking a risk like this and I did feel a level of vulnerability, as there was no-one to support it for me as Kenny was working on something else. It crossed my mind as whether to say anything, but a momentary feeling of embarrassment and an element of peer pressure, stopped me from speaking up. "I'll be okay," I told myself - "these things only happen to other people," that comforted me as I climbed the rungs, to join Keith on the rooftop.

Sure enough, we were finished within the hour with two of us on the job, brilliant - time to go home. I envisioned warming myself up with a hot bath followed by a beer or two and seeing the kids before they went to bed. Kenny had re-joined us and he supported the ladder as I made my way back onto the ground. Kenny started to load up our van with our tools. I was about to hold the ladder for Keith to descent, when he called me back up to collect a bucket of tools. As I went back up the ladder, I muttered to myself how I shouldn't be doing that unaided again and really, I ought to have been watching Nottingham Forest play. I was about halfway back up, and suddenly, without realising what was happening, I was gone - off the ladder in a split second. I landed with a thud, without fully realising what had just happened as it happened so quickly. As I reached out to touch my head, I was instantly panicked as I noticed that my fingers were covered in blood. As I screamed out, Keith scrambled down the ladder and Kenny appeared at my other side, both staring down at me with horrified expressions etched on their faces. "Bloody hell Jase, are you ok?" asked Keith with a concerned tone.

As I tried to move my legs, in that second, I felt terror as it dawned on me that I could not feel a thing in my legs. I let out a bloodcurdling shriek at that stark realisation. "I can't feel my fucking legs! Help me, fucking help me!" I tried to move my lower body again, but nothing happened, I could not feel anything. Oh my God, what the hell had I done?

7
The Aftermath

Kenny crouched down beside me in the tight space, I was trapped in-between two walls. Keith asked me again if I was alright and then yelled that he was going to call for an ambulance, his words trailing off as he got up and ran off. I could hear myself screaming but it felt surreal. Was this actually happening to me? Bloody hell, what on earth was going to happen? I was freaking myself out and Kenny could sense my increasing fear, as he was frantically trying to reassure me and calm me down. He grabbed my hand, squeezing it and in his eyes, as he was over me, I could see terror. So he was telling me to calm down but he was actually terrified himself? In that moment, I feared the absolute worst - I was never going to be able to use my legs again. I felt sick rising in my throat which I forced back down and tears streamed down my face. Kenny placed his jacket over me as it was bitterly cold, especially on the hard ground. I was in a lot of achy pain as I had winded myself, then told myself I was going to be okay. I HAD to be. I had kids, I had a future. Thinking of Sam and Abbi made it worse, as I thought of them seeing me like this, pathetically lying on the floor, panicking and not being able to move. "Get a grip Jason," I shouted internally, "be strong for God's sake."

Looking up and around me, the narrow gap between the two buildings was dark and getting darker as it started to become a little dusky. It almost felt as though I was in my coffin, the sheer walls either side of me and I was bound in a tight space. For a fleeting moment, I asked myself if I had died and this was all in my spirit's vision. With two faces looking over at me, I thought, was I dead? Keith's loud voice on the scene jolted me back into reality. "The ambulance is on it's way Jase!"

I felt a glimmer of hope at his tense words. They both held a hand each at the awkward angle we were in, I calmed down a little as they were constantly talking to me, attempting to soothe me and even make light of the situation. It helped a little. It seemed ages until the ambulance arrived, as though time had stood still. My heart was pounding in my chest, I still felt sick and had the acrid bile taste in my mouth.

Then I heard the sounds of sirens in the distance, oh my God - they were here to rescue me. It made me cry again, feeling sorry for myself whilst wondering how the hell this had happened. That bloody ladder, I must have lost my footing. So much for it happening to someone else. Kenny jumped up as the sirens were close to flag them over to where we were.

They were able to drive right up to where I lay, the sirens quietened, heavy doors slammed open and shut and I heard footsteps running towards me. A pair of unfamiliar faces peered down at me, and a masculine deep voice said surprisingly calmly, "okay Jason, what have we here then? I'd like you to remain as calm and still as possible, and we are going to help you, okay?" The voice was a bit muffled and seemed so far away from me.

Still? I thought - I wouldn't be going anywhere soon. My mind raced and I uttered some words to them both. They discussed my situation with one another in a speedy assessment and fast came to the conclusion that because the space I was in was so tight, they were not able to get into me with a stretcher. More soothing words, but I could see the look of worry on Kenny and Keith's faces, which worried me more. Being told that I was going to be alright was hard to swallow as I lay there feeling helpless and anything but alright. I desperately wanted to believe them and felt a glimmer of hope. I knew I had to be.

Suddenly it seemed so much colder, and I shivered intensely. One of the ambulance people covered me with an extra blanket she grabbed from the vehicle. They suspected that I had suffered a spinal injury and without more information about the depth of my injuries, they were reluctant to move me in case it caused subsequent damage. They'd radioed a paramedic team for specialist advice and we were waiting for them to arrive on the scene. We waited for what seemed like hours but was not, and they contacted the paramedics again, however, they were about an hour away, which was far from ideal. In the end they had no choice but to move me, as I was getting colder and they could not leave me waiting for attention any longer. From the ambulance, they emerged with a spinal board. It was a big struggle with no space to move me barely, but somehow they shoved my dead weight onto the board. I was a six footer, so not a small frame for them to shift. I was just relieved for something to be happening as it made me feel more hopeful. I shuddered from the cold, which had gone through to my bones, but also when I was laying on a trolley in the ambulance, I knew I still could not feel anything in my legs. I briefly panicked outwardly again, screamed out, hyperventilating and was given some oxygen to help me to calm down and breathe properly.

The lads said their concerned goodbyes and told me they'd meet me at the hospital after going to fetch Paula on the way. Halfway to Queen's Medical Centre, we met the paramedics. We stopped for a couple of brief moments as they pulled by the roadside and I was transferred over, wheeling me on a trolley on the board. Once inside the other vehicle, my breathing was checked, my heart was monitored and I was once more reassured.

On arrival at the A&E department of the huge hospital in Nottingham, we moved swiftly. I was pulled out of the paramedic's vehicle, onto a trolley and pushed quickly through the automatic doors. It felt surreal, as I was rushed along the corridors, seeing a blur of lights and sounds as they wheeled me into a room. It instantly smelt of hospital. That distinct, medicinal odour in my nostrils. I heard lots of new voices as I was rigged up with monitors and other machines attached to parts of my body, including my fingers which were still felt freezing cold. The questions began, it felt like I was fired at with one after another and I was so tense. Pulling at my clothing so that they could get to my injuries, I raged from within as there was no way they were going to cut off my favourite Adidas hoody, it was my football top but had no zip. I shouted out and told them to leave it alone, followed by asking what the football score was! Even in this state, it crossed my mind that my team were playing and that if I had been there, this would never have happened. That thought made me angrier still, strapped helplessly to the spinal board, freaking out at not being able to move or feel my legs. I was ushered to quieten down as I wasn't helping anyone by being so vocal. It's alright for them I thought, they were not the one laying here in distress.

I was taken off for an x-ray. I was unstrapped from the board and moved across to the large x-ray machine. On my own, my mind still racing with all kinds of thoughts, I felt both reassured that they were doing something and petrified of what they might find at the same time. Tightening my fists, my fingernails dug into my hands, not feeling the pain. The procedure was soon over and I was wheeled into a side waiting room. Still on my own, not knowing what to think and still sore at the realisation of my hoody being ripped open. Then through the door, appeared the consultant, with a big smile planted on his face. My heart raced and my eyes lit up, there's no way he'd be smiling if it was bad news. Oh my God, I was going to be okay - just like they said! As his white coated figure neared me, he revealed that they could not see anything on the x-ray, there were no breaks in my vertebrae but that I was experiencing a spinal shock condition. He further explained, that this is when a person experiences a really bad trauma to the point of losing their sensation, their spine swells which causes the damage, but it settles back down and when it does, the sensation returns. It could take a couple of hours, or be a matter of days or weeks, it varied on each individual. I heaved a massive sigh of relief and actually shed a few tears and thanked him profusely. I felt extremely lucky and the thought of it happening only to, 'other people,' returned. I couldn't wait to see my family and share the good news, well and the bad I suppose, with them.

As I lay there alone, I smiled and promised myself that I was going to go and see my team play again, after something like this, it had shocked me so much and you never, ever knew what was around the corner. A few minutes later the doctor returned and said that just to be on the safe side, they wanted to send me for a CT scan, as it was a little more detailed, just to ensure that they hadn't missed anything. I nodded, thought nothing of it and felt glad that they were being so thorough with me. As I was wheeled to the scan room, I had much happier thoughts of seeing my kids, of football and enjoying a pint or two at the pub to celebrate. Again, this test did not take long, and I was taken back to the same waiting area. Not long before I see Paula and the kids I thought to myself. A few minutes later, the same doctor returned, this time with a very different expression. My heart lurched. Then very matter of fact, he proceeded to explain to me that the scan had showed up a fracture, this had caused massive spinal injuries and that I'd never walk again. Just like that. Then he left the room, with no real bedside manner, leaving me in utter disbelief. Had I just heard him correctly? I would never walk again? What? That could not possibly be right? What the hell!

On reflection, I've always said that my wife was there when I was informed, but actually I was on my own, I heard it but I almost didn't, as I was in such shock. I'd been terrified for a couple or so hours since it happened and expecting the worst, then to be told by a consultant, a medical expert, that I was actually going to be okay, well the relief was enormous. It was as though it was the biggest weight you could possibly imagine had been lifted off of me and I was granted a life again. Then only half an hour or so later, to be told my worst case scenario was actually true, and that the amazing conversation thirty minutes ago was not the truth, was more than I could take. It was unfathomable, impossible for me to take on board.

Paula was devastated when she was told, but she actually kept her calm and tried her best to reassure me. She kept it together really well and I even asked her if she'd remembered to record the football match. Can you believe it? I thought initially, "that's it then, my marriage is definitely over now," but her response made me wonder if actually we would get through it, as trauma can actually bring some people closer together.

My mum responded differently and screamed out loud when the same doctor spoke to her and my dad in the same, unemotional manner, she was my mum after all. Apparently the medical staff have to remain detached, professional and cannot get involved.

A day later, on the Monday, I had to have a major operation, under general anaesthetic. This raised my hopes, as they were giving me treatment, which could give me a good result. I felt groggy from the anaesthetic as I came around from the operation. All it had done was to put two titanium rods and 4 screws in my back to stabilise my spine. It was a matter of course, not some miracle cure. I was in denial as even though I'd been told that I wouldn't walk again, I discovered that the medics were only making presumptions because of the nature of my injury and that they couldn't guarantee exactly what would happen as every case was different. I think everyone can recall hearing of a story where someone has defeated the odds and regained their mobility.

As my accident had been of such a traumatic nature, the original ambulance driver came to visit me a couple of days later, after spending quite a bit of time waiting with me at the time of the accident. He was expecting to hear good news, and his face scrunched up, devastated, when he found out my outcome. They must see so many accidents and get a good idea of the prognosis and I could tell he was genuinely shocked.

The days of that week all blurred into one, trauma has that effect and the shock knocked all of my family and friends. It was the unexpected, it really was the story that you only heard about other people and not someone close to you. I was drip fed morphine with a clicker to cope with the pain of the operation. Friends and family all came to visit me with cards, but people were at a loss of what to say to me, it felt very awkward, and I didn't know what to say in return. Paula brought the children in to see me which made me very emotional and I cried my eyes out. What had I done to their little lives? I felt so guilty and felt sad for myself, as I imagined not being able to play with them like a 'normal' dad.

My entire life had been tipped upside down, inside out and would never be the same again. On the last ward visit from my consultant I was under, he informed me that I was being transferred to a specialist spinal unit at the end of the week.

8
Lodge Moore Acute Ward

By Friday of that week, as promised, I had been transferred via ambulance to a specialist rehabilitation unit in Sheffield, *Lodge Moore*. Admissions were always on Fridays apparently. When I arrived in the communal lounge area, the film, *The Commitments* was showing, I could identify it was that movie from the lively soul tunes in full force blasting out of the television. I'd seen that a couple of years previously when it was released. Most of the patients were sitting around drinking cans of beer, which surprised me at first. It seemed ages since I'd tasted beer. Someone came over to me and said hello, it felt surreal and was a very overwhelming time.

Throughout the UK, there were only nine of these specialist spinal units and where you ended up depended on which catchment area you lived in, this was closest to me. At first, each patient had to spend a few weeks or so on the acute ward, determined by your level of injury. I was measured for a big brace, then a plaster cast of my body was created to mould the brace on. Once the brace was ready, I had to wear it all of the time, which left me feeling trussed up like a chicken and was very restrictive. I was turned every three hours in bed to change my position, the nursing staff manually moving me, to prevent me getting bed sores. This was continued for 24 hours a day, and it was hard to sleep being disturbed frequently and stuck in the brace. Even going for a shower, a regular every day task, I had to stay flat on my back. All my of my inhibitions vanished, I had been plunged into relying on the nurses to do everything for me, even the toileting. It was humiliating all the same and I envisioned myself as a helpless child. I felt pathetic and so angry. To actually go to the toilet, I had to have some medicine injected into me and I had to do it on the bed. Can you imagine that? The smell was horrendous and it was really degrading. I was staying on the acute ward and I never got used to it.

For me that meant four weeks of having to lay flat on my bed. After that stage, you progressed through to the main rehabilitation section of the unit. The people drinking that night in the lounge, had been off of their backs for a couple of months to be able to sit like that and watch tv. I compared myself, would I ever reach that stage?

My injury was a complete break, known in the medical world as T10. The T9-T12 vertebrae form the base of the thoracic spine, and this comprises of 12 segments between the lumbar and cervical levels. Depending on how complete the spinal cord damage is determines the severity of injury and the likeliness of recovery. Although mine was not good news at all, my mind was in constant conflict. Half of me felt surges of positivity and hope whilst the other part of me felt the deep loss and was silently grieving. The mental effects were harrowing as well, it was much more than just a physical trauma. Each time I dared to explore the possibility that I may get my feelings back, it was dashed with the opposing idea of me being one of the truly unlucky ones. You can possibly imagine the rollercoaster journey, as visitors would occasionally bring in a leaflet about spinal surgery, or someone would excitedly share some news of a brand new miracle that they had heard about in another country. False hope was devastating I fast came to realise. I was initially approached in hospital by a legal person and I was told that my case was very complex and that they would try and look at it.

It was an endless four weeks, on that acute ward. I was only with three other patients who also had to have complete bed rest with nothing more to do than lay and stare at the ceiling for weeks on end, and I received a constant stream of visitors each day. My mate Sean, would pick up all my mates up in a transit van, they'd drink on the way over, as they were apprehensive about seeing me. I'd feel the same and drink a couple of cans before they came, then they'd sit round my bed and say everything apart from what they really wanted to say. It was a very bleak time for me as there was so much time to think and my thoughts were often very depressing once my visitors had gone home. I was prescribed a course of sleeping tablets to help me to get the rest my body needed. Just like in the big hospital, I was turned every three hours, day and night. I remember feeling desperate to get out of that area, onto the rehab ward and to be working towards getting home, if there was to be any hope in resurrecting my marriage. It was agonising, and I felt swamped with sorrow and fears. I was also terrified that I may lose my kids, it was hard to be positive in my situation.

After four weeks of rest, I was allowed to move. It was daunting but I was excited also and felt such a sense of relief as I really didn't think that I could last much longer laying like that, my mind was in such a bad place. My aunty Jenny and uncle Terry were visiting me when I first sat up. It may sound simple, but even sitting up was an ordeal. My head immediately spun, and I remained dizzy with the room whirling at a fast pace for twenty minutes and had to lay back down. I could have cried. The second time was better, and with a slightly dazed head, two of the nurses lifted me out of the bed with a hoist and for the first time, sat me in a wheelchair. It was a huge cumbersome thing, very typical of the NHS. The one thought that struck me instantly was that I had gone from being a six foot bloke to being what must have been, 3-4 foot in this chair. It was a completely different view for a start, how bizarre. I hated it but at the same time I was grateful for it to enable me to get out of my bed and be mobile. Surely this was not going to be my destiny forever? I pushed that depressing thought away. I was instructed on how to make the chair move and it was far harder than I thought it would be. Not only was the chair itself heavy, I had to move my weight also. This was really going to take some getting used to, and part of me did not want to. That continued conflict.

Aunty Jenny, Uncle Terry and I slowly made our way to the canteen, I felt so self-conscious as though everyone was staring at me, even though all of the patients were in the same boat. It was horrible. Jenny was really kind and supportive but when we reached the counter in the café area, the catering assistant dismissed me, not even looking at me, and asked Jenny what I'd like to drink. It's hard to explain how that moment made me feel. Not only was I in this state but I was now invisible as well and not deemed capable of answering a simple question. It was insulting and I felt like a child. Is this what my life had come to?

It was traumatising to be reliant on a wheelchair, especially as I had been such an active and sporty person before my accident. The daily frustrations intensified depending on my mood each day. We all heard of the miracle stories and I tried my hardest to convince myself that I would be the next one. If I didn't have that hope to cling on to, what would I have? There was no proper emotional support on the unit which I dearly needed, so had to find it within myself and from my family and friends. The closest advice I got was from my social worker, but that was more focussed on organising what benefits I was now entitled to and what would happen on my discharge. I was asked how I felt but I always put on a brave face and found it impossible to speak truthfully about my inner demons. I didn't want to put my problems onto anyone else, always the protector. I knew how impactful words could be and the last thing I wanted was to be more of a hindrance than I had already become.

From the moment you arrived at the unit to the day you left, it was geared up to you leaving and becoming as independent as possible. I knew that I'd be there up to around the six-month mark average. My time on the acute ward was over, as my doctor informed me that I was ready to transfer to the rehab ward. I didn't know whether to smile or to cry to be honest.

9
Rehab

Once I was through to the rehab ward, everything was based on your physical and fitness state. I was supported on what were, simple tasks to someone able bodied, such as getting out of bed, getting into a bath, having a shower, cooking and then wheelchair skills. It surprised me how rigorous and structured it was. Each day was the same disciplined routine - at 7am the lights went on and you had an hour to get yourself ready, which could be a rush when it included going to the toilet, breakfast, going to the gym, Occupational Therapy, wheelchair training, lunch, the gym again, swimming, all designed to build up your upper body strength and to get you into as peak a state of fitness as possible. The meals were healthy foods to aid this process.

I'll never forget the day when my consultant came to see me, and in his stern tone, delivered me the news that I was doubly incontinent. What exactly did he mean by that? When the reality hit home, and the realisation of what that meant for the rest of my life, I was devastated, I sobbed as soon as he had left the room. It was the hardest thing for me to accept out of everything I had been through, more so than not walking. My muscles and nerves in my lower regions had suffered such intense trauma through my fall, that the damage to that area was permanent and there was nothing that could reverse it. It did nothing for my manliness and any dignity I may have been grasping onto with all of my might, vanished in that moment. I was really shocked at the news that I'd never be able to function normally again with my bowels or my urinary system. It was instantly degrading. It had been bad enough with the toileting as it was but I thought it would improve over time. Up until this point my bodily functions had been dealt with by the nurses on the bed. I didn't actually have to do anything myself, just to get on with it and then they would come and clean me up and that was it. That was unpleasant enough and left you feeling helpless. A short while later, a nurse appeared with a pair of rubber gloves and a suppository, not the most welcoming sight at the end of your bed. At first I had to get accustomed to applying this myself in the bed, before progressing onto using proper facilities. For quite a while it was very traumatic as you had no control over what your body needed to do but eventually you got more in tune with your body's needs. My bowels were all over the place in shock from the trauma to my body and having accidents became a regular thing, much to my embarrassment. I would start to feel I had it under better control and then I'd be in the gym or somewhere else and I would soil myself. There's nothing as degrading to a human as this, it was reminiscent of my baby days, horrible. Then I would feel a hundred times worse and as though I'd gone backwards again. The more it happened, the more normal it felt however, and it wasn't exclusive to me, the other patients had to go through the same humiliating experience. To cope with it, we all used to laugh, whoever's turn it was. It was tinged with shame from us all and we all felt for one another. Each morning we were given just half an hour to go to the toilet, which often was not long enough and I felt pressured to get the deed done which never helped. That's usually when an accident occurred. The unit stocked a very strong deodorant which successfully masked the smell, but it was far from subtle. I'd see a patient go to their bed, the curtains would be drawn around them and then after a while the waft of this deodorant would fill the air and everyone knew what they had just done. Everyone was going through their own private hell. You really do become a changed person.

Going for a wee was not much better, horrendous actually, especially in the early days. I was given a sheath to wear, which drained through to a plastic bag it is attached to, that is discreetly worn underneath your clothing. When the bag is full it gets emptied and I did get used to it, I had no choice mind you. It's called a Convene. Back then, they were not as well fitted, and when I went to the pub, it would often blow off and I would wet myself. These were still a vast improvement to the home made versions that people had to use just a decade previously, so I considered myself lucky in this respect.

The unit was such a safe environment and definitely cushioned us all from the harsh real world outside of the hospital doors. It was flat for a start and once you began to venture outside you realised just how many obstacles there are when you are not using your own legs. The staff actively encouraged us to socialise, which involved, drinking and going to the pub. This was something I did look forward to at the end of a testing day. After dinner each evening, most of us in rehab would sit around in our chairs drinking cans of beer, with relatively animated discussions on what each of us would do when we left. None of us really knew what to truly expect as it was unknown territory. This whole experience was the unknown. It must have looked comical to an observer when we all filed out to the local pub. It was situated on the top of a big hill on the moors of all places, and there were two nurses running around after us and pushing us uphill. So there would have been about ten wheelchairs all lined up in the dark, making their way to the pub. I did feel embarrassed to start with, being out in public in that bloody chair. It didn't do a lot for a young bloke's self-esteem, but I knew that we all had to get used to it and be integrated back into society away from the comfort of the unit. It would be easy to become institutionalised and reliant on that place and the people. My mates were allowed to take me to the pub, they put me and the chair in the van, get me drunk and bring me back. The nurses instructions were - we had to be back at 10pm, as doors were locked, but we would stay until last orders (of course!), then they were so scared of the nurses, they'd take me through the back door, ring the night bell, run off and leave me there.

There was some competitiveness surrounding the range of wheelchairs, as when you were having to use the great big ones at first, you couldn't help but feel a bit envious of the more modern, slimline versions that some of the other patients were in. It wasn't quite upgrading to the newest car model but that feeling was there all the same. It was a skill to learn how to properly use one and to manoeuvre it up and down curbs, around tight corners and all of the other challenges that I had previously taken for granted. If you fell out, which did happen (and not just when I'd had beer!), you had to learn how to haul yourself back in if there was no one else around to help you. You feel like a stuntman in some ways and do learn to wheel with care. Farndon FC and pub did a fundraiser whilst I was in hospital, and bought me my first chair, there were lots of cuts on my head from falling out of the chair!

I got on well with all of the medical staff; we were a close-knit community and it was like living in another world for several months. I had an Occupational Therapist that was originally allocated to me. She was a young, newly qualified girl and I was one of the first patients that she had looked after by herself. However, Paula could not stand her and I'm sure she had pangs of jealousy at the close relationship that was building. I had to rely on this therapist to help me with most tasks and spent many hours with her. Over time, I was getting attached to her, it was hard not to with the type of closeness the relationship demanded. It became the highlight of my day, when she would come in to give me my physio exercise in my bed. I was craving human connection and that contact made my day. When we went out to the pub, it would be this particular therapist that pushed me up that steep hill. It was easy to see how relationships did form between staff and patients, you heard of it, as close bonds are made. Sometimes it felt as though she was the only person that really understood what I was going through. The staff were aware of my strained and deteriorating marriage, and wanting to support me with this aspect, they took my Occupational Therapist off of me and I worked closely with Sharman instead. Sharman was in charge of the OT department. Nothing was said to me at the time and I just got on with it. In my heart, I knew it was a positive move to protect me.

Paula came to visit me every day when I was in the acute ward, she was actually very supportive, quite a rock despite our issues. Our kids were so young, they couldn't understand why daddy was in this strange bed and not at home. Now I was in rehab I didn't get as many visitors, including my wife, as I was busy all day, every day. I was always hearing some of the other patients say, that were further on in their rehab and having home visits, how bad things were at home. Partners were leaving them as they couldn't cope with the demands of having a disabled partner and the life change, or their marriage was already on the rocks. It was a well-known fact, that if you had problems before your accident, you would probably not last a year. It sounded harsh and I knew I fell into that category, it worried me sick. Picturing Abbi and Sam's little faces broke my heart. At about halfway through my stay, Paula came in one day, and out of the blue, suggested that we all move away once I'd got out, and that a fresh start was exactly what we needed to move forward. It struck me as odd, this sudden remark that came from nowhere, it was not as though we'd previously discussed it and she was so sure about it. I explained that I couldn't possibly move away as I'd need my friends and family now more than ever. As I mulled it over in my mind, I had a realisation of what this was really about, something had happened, my gut instinct knew. I had encouraged her to go out one Saturday night, as we all had a drink on the ward and that she deserved a break after coming to see me so frequently. She agreed and she went out, however she never came in the following day either which was totally out of character. That had niggled me a lot and I knew there was a reason and that she could not face me. She knew there and then that there was no future in our marriage, as I was going to find out she'd cheated on me. It was all going to come out and by moving away from the area and everyone that we knew, she could avoid that confrontation and continue to live a lie. It hit me like a ton of bricks, even though neither of us said a word about it, we both knew in our hearts. We'd become exactly as the other people in couples on this ward, just as they had predicted.

The physical demands were tough, there were no shortcuts to convalescence. My upper body was actually in the fittest condition I'd ever been in and I needed that to help myself survive each day. The gym and physio really took it out of me and my arm muscles bulked up considerably. A small silver lining.

All of the patients were friendly, despite their varying states of health but one element I found hard to deal with was that they were laughing, joking and drinking a lot of the time. I'd be in the communal areas, sitting quietly trying to read and focus on something to distract me, and I'd suddenly hear loud bellows of laughter and equally loud jokes being shared over a few tinnies. All I could think of was how my life was in turmoil, there was no going back and quite frankly, what the hell was there to laugh about? I was aware that I kept my distance a little and really only befriended one person, David. He was similar to me, a young lad, although not married, he loved his art too and his business was as an artist. I spent hours with him at his bedside, keeping one another company. I empathised deeply with David, as he had been on a last minute holiday with his brother and on the first day, he had dived into the swimming pool and seconds later had broken his neck. He was not even have supposed to have gone on the holiday and was tagging along to fill a space. The poor guy. His accident had left him paralysed from the neck down and he needed a ventilator to help his lungs to breathe. I felt guilty for thinking it, but I was grateful for at least having the use of my arms, to not have that was unimaginable. We built a strong bond over the weeks as we shared experiences and I held his beer for him so that he could drink it through a straw. He went on to learn how to paint holding the brush in his mouth, it was astonishing and just goes to show what a person can achieve if they are pushed to their limits, or have their options taken away. What an amazing young man and it felt a privilege to be his friend. One day an ex-patient came in to visit the unit, as they sometimes did. I guess after spending so long there and forming the bonds with the staff that you do it was understandable. This particular chap had turned to alcohol to cope each day. It both shocked me and it didn't shock me. Everyone needs a release, especially when faced with such adversity and this was this person's crutch. Who was I to judge?

Then there was the sex education talk. Point blank, I refused as I just could not face this. I just was not ready to hear it at that time. I felt so sensitive about it and it was too humiliating and not something I had to face, like the toileting aspects. I could live without this for now. I recalled the stories from the other male patients as they revealed how bad their sex lives had become at home and that their girlfriends had left them. It painted a pretty bleak picture for me and I just knew Paula and I wouldn't cope with that on top of everything else. In the end, the staff gently advised me to return home when the time came, rebuild my life and when the time was right for me, to come back and we would have the conversation then. That seemed a much better option.

Further on during my rehab journey, I had some driving lessons as driving a regular car was no longer an option. I had to get used to using hand controls to power and steer the car which was another challenge in itself, but being able to continue to drive was really important to me as I had already lost so much.

Adjacent to the unit, there was a small building which was fitted out as an adapted house. Towards the end of my stay, I was encouraged to stay in there for a weekend with my family. It was a strange experience but we all coped with it and I managed well. After that I was allowed to go home for weekends as a practice for when I was discharged. Also on a Friday, patients would leave and new patients would be admitted. Each week, I had to attend a ward round with all the staff that were responsible for my care and in front of you, they would discuss your case and decide if you were ready to leave or not. It was something I got worked up about each time, as whatever they decided would either give you the chance to get out or keep you there for another week. I felt under pressure from Paula and from myself to leave and give our marriage a chance. I was clutching at straws as I felt we were doomed deep down and it was as though time was running out. It was only because of my own childhood that I was so fiercely determined that it wasn't going to happen to my family. If you didn't have hope though, what did you have?

10
Homeward Bound

The Friday that I was discharged from the rehab unit was a myriad of emotions for me. The past four months had been a rollercoaster ride for me that had all been leading up to this special day. I didn't actually know how I'd feel until the day came round and it was a combination of fear and excitement. The unit and its safe parameters had become my home and I saw how patients can become institutionalised, with the daily schedules and closed environment. Even though I'd had my home visits, I always knew that I was returning to the safe confines of the unit, which was a comfort especially when I was feeling at a particularly low ebb.

Some of my close friends collected me and my belongings and I was issued my prescribed drugs and a prescription for my next batch. Anything to make my life easier to what it was going to be on the outside. I know everyone was concerned about how I was going to cope day to day. Although I was apprehensive I felt sure I would manage. I still had a high level of fitness and strength in my upper body which I needed to do most things and the unit had nurtured me to feel equipped to carry out daily activities confidently. Even though our house had not been adapted for a wheelchair, we had put certain measures in place for when I'd visited. We had a ramp installed so I could enter the house through a side door, the front door was out of the question. The double bed had been shifted downstairs and placed in the front room, making it more of a bed sit than a lounge and as I couldn't access the toilet upstairs easily, we had a commode which was kept in the corridor that led from inside towards the outside of the building. To have a weekly bath, which was upstairs in the bathroom, I would bump up and down our staircase and Paula was going to help me in the bath itself. The plan was in place, now to see what the reality would be like.

Arriving home was emotional and the kids were very excited to see daddy home after all of this time. Abbi was prancing around the front room, giggling and smiling and Sam was happily gurgling away, the happy baby that he was, and starting to chatter. Paula seemed pleased to have me there and for a split second it seemed idyllic. This is how it should be I thought to myself, altogether again at home. This was short lived however, as within half an hour Paula declared that she was going out on her own that night. Her words hit me like a rock, I knew we were far from being alright, but for her to go out on my first night back home felt very harsh and my momentary illusion was shattered.

Everybody was aware of my marital problems, family, friends and acquaintances. It was a close community and word gets around. Nobody actually said anything to me or Paula though, it was quite bizarre, a façade masked our own despair. And alcohol, that helped enormously, albeit temporarily. So as Paula went out, so did I. At the pub anyone and everyone wanted to buy me a drink. I knew they were pleased to see me back at the local again but they were walking on eggshells some of them, not really sure what to say to me. I felt a little uncomfortable too for their discomfort and my shame that I felt for being in a wheelchair. I'd always fantasised about wanting to be, "different," when I was younger, in my mod days, and now look at me, blatantly standing out from the crowd. Now I desperately longed to fit in, how ironic. I eagerly accepted the rounds of drinks, starting on beers and progressing onto vodka's. Not single shots though, but doubles and trebles. As the evening wore on, I slowly lapsed into a drunken stupor. Yes, there were laughs and some drunken pub banter, but I was empty inside when I had those seconds that my mind drifted back into my reality. I made out to everyone that I was okay, doing my protective act again, I couldn't verbalise how I really felt and knew that people did not want to really know or would understand me. It was easier this way, there was enough to cope with as it was. The effects of alcohol changed from jollying me along to me ending up in a blubbering mess. Friends took me home, and arriving home to an empty house hit me like a ton of bricks, and I broke down, Paula wasn't coming home that night, my first night back. The kids were with her aunty. No-one there. I thought about the unit and in that moment wished I was back there. Seeing me in the state I was in, my friends would not leave me. We stayed up chatting and I even drank some more, I just needed to blot it all out and make it go away. Eventually I fell into a drink induced heavy sleep, a couple of my mates watching over me, I could make out the blurry outline of their faces as my eyes shut.

The banging headache the following morning was not helping me, I looked around the room and spotted evidence that two of my mates had crashed out on the sofa and floor. Paracetamols, I needed paracetamols and a mug of tea. As if he'd read my mind, my mate walked into the room, hearing me stir, with a steaming mug of tea and a box of painkillers. I felt depressed and hungover but also grateful, very grateful that my mates had been there with me. My situation came right back into my mind. God, what was I going to do?

By lunchtime, Paula arrived home, also looking a bit worse for wear. Before we had chance to start a conversation, she announced that she was leaving, just like that. I swallowed hard, gulping, and asked her to repeat what she had just said. As I heard the same sentence I felt my anger rise, like a hot volcano about to explode. She looked sheepish as my face glowered at hers. I felt my cheeks reddening, a sweat breaking out and a deep growl forming in my throat. There was a deathly silence before I heard the loudest sound I had ever made leave my vocal chords, like a loud roar. She instantly matched my shout out and seconds later we were engaged in an almighty slanging match. It was horrible and we hurled some hurtful words at one another. Both of us now crying, this was the final nail in the coffin, there was no going back from this. She stormed upstairs and I heard her ransacking the rooms, scrabbling around to grab her belongings and clothing for the kids. I sat in my chair and sobbed. My immediate thought was that I would lose the kids and that was too painful to bear. I pushed the thought away. My mind was racing, flitting between what was happening right now, what the future would hold and what I had suspected for quite some time. Suddenly it all fell into place and made sense. I'd had a sneaking feeling that she had been seeing someone else when I was in the unit, and it was a stubborn thought that wouldn't shift. That Sunday when she hadn't come to see me had made me feel sick to the core but nothing to what I felt now. My fear was confirmed. When I'd been in the unit, she'd had an affair. I knew that my accident and all that had happened since had impacted so many of the lives of people around me. I felt so guilty for that and it gnawed away at me daily. Obviously Paula's life would have been changed most of all, and in her weaker moments she'd found some comfort with someone else. It wasn't a legitimate excuse but I got it on some level. If things had been the other way around, I think I would have probably have done the same, plus I knew full well that we were on shaky ground. We never stood a chance.

As I heard the front door slam, I knew she would not be coming back, it was over. That was it, I hit the alcohol and in a short space of time I had friends come round. The more vodka that I consumed the angrier and sadder I felt. Throughout the course of that day and evening I didn't stop drinking. Sometimes it's as though you can drink and drink and not feel drunk, this was one of those times. I was furiously attempting to force the raw pain down and push it away. My mates had known about the affair but had kept it all under wraps in an attempt to protect me. They rallied round me and were such a tower of strength to me when I needed it badly. The alcohol reached me later that night, as I disappeared into a tearful drunken sleep.

11
Depression

I never would have made it without those close friends at that point. They were there for me the whole time, through thick and thin, with their amazing loyalty and care. I discovered the meaning of the term true friendship as acquaintances became close connections and they provided me with such a solid support to get through the daily struggle I found myself in. I am grateful from the bottom of my heart to all of those friends but especially to Niall, Tim, Colin and Stewart who became my four core friends. Without fail, one of them would always be present, which was a big undertaking on their behalf. I didn't ask, they insisted, as they saw the worsening psychological state I was in. With my heavy drinking came drunken outbursts and in those moments I would sometimes say careless remarks, really not caring about my outcome. I wasn't suicidal, as I think it takes a lot to cross that line, where you see nothing but darkness with no light of hope, but I didn't care about myself. My behaviour was reckless and showed no signs of improving, outside of the time I spent with my kids. It was my letting off steam time where I did not have to hold it together. My family were torn seeing me in that impetuous mindset, I was no longer the Jason they knew me as. As much as they hated it, I couldn't stop myself. Sharon, my sister, was a constant help, not judging me or telling me what I should or shouldn't do but she was just there to listen, or to make me laugh and jolly me up at a situation that just was not funny.

Knowing that my marriage was over, I went to see a solicitor to file for a divorce. Paula had got there before me, so I had to find another to represent me. Apparently she was leaving me for my unreasonable behaviour - my being in a wheelchair. That made it sound as though it was a choice I had made. I was advised not to fight her case of unreasonable behaviour, but to accept it.

A week after coming home, my closest friend came round to see me on his own. He confessed to the fling he'd had with Paula. This was not a stranger but my best mate, oh my God, that was the worst kind of betrayal. I hit the roof and went ballistic but then soon calmed down. It was something I knew deep down, but hearing him say it was like a red rag to a bull. In my calmer moments after my rage, I just knew that I had to accept it. What was the point of staying angry? It would punish me even more and right now I could not handle anything else. Besides, I'd lost my marriage, the use of my legs, and my life as it was, I sure as hell wasn't prepared to lose my best mate. I had enough insight to understand why it happened.

It had not lasted for long and Paula had already moved on after she'd realised this affair was going to come out, she'd met someone else on one of her night's out whilst I was in the unit. In fact, I saw Paula with this guy around this time. I was in town with my mates in the daytime when I spotted them across the street, with my kids. I was distraught to think that Abbi and Sam would start to view this stranger as their dad and replace me. It broke my heart to see them altogether and before I knew what I was doing, my anger took over and I began shouting across to them and started to wheel myself furiously in their direction. They caught sight of me and I saw their pained expressions as they glanced down at the kids and back at each other and then me, then they themselves picked up speed and tried to hurry Abbi and Sam along. This gave me chance to get nearer initially and my rage fuelled me onwards. My mates called me and ran alongside me urging me to stop. I refused to listen and charged on in my chair, dodging people that were getting in my way on the pavement. I followed them for quite a while, angrily chasing them across town but as I tired they got further away. Stalling to a stop and a heavy sigh, I broke down and felt such a fool. They were tears of frustration too, as it was the first time that it really hit home that I couldn't do what I wanted to do in a situation.

Drinking became my crutch and I always said I was okay, rarely showing how I really felt, feeling the pressure of holding it all in. As the weeks went by, the drinking spiralled more out of control, all I wanted to do outside of seeing the kids, was to get slaughtered and block everything out. I saw Paula from time to time under duress, I was so angry with her for hurting me as much as she had. She came round to help me have my weekly bath for a few weeks, probably out of guilt than any feelings for me. However I was grateful as it was a real struggle at first. Paula's sister, Lisa, became a close confidante and I would just share thoughts of how I was feeling and acting, and again she never judged me, just listened.

The arrangement that we had was that Abbi came to stop with me Monday to Thursday, whilst Sam would just visit, or I would visit him. Paula was living at her sister, Shelly's house in the village. He was so young and too much of a handful for me to cope with on my own for any period. My balance wasn't that good to even hold him on my lap. I wanted to see him as much as possible though, which reverted back to my own insecurity as a child. I put all of my focus onto the kids and the downside was when they were not there and with their mum. The stress levels were massive for me. I was not really in a fit state to look after her but I was adamant that I could cope. My mum and dad were amazing and supported me so much.

As soon as Abbi left on a Thursday, I'd hit the bottle again, using the vodka to numb my overwhelming pain. I'd drink mainly at the pub, then carry on afterwards at home. A friend would always stayover and they all rotated in shifts to keep me company.

By the July, my friend Sean had moved out of his flat on the same street as me and into a house. It was an ideal situation for me to be able to transfer into the council flat which I went on to have adapted. This made day to day living a bit easier.

I saw my GP as my mood was so low, and after thrusting a prescription for anti-depressants into my hand, telling me to pull myself together, he informed me that I'd be okay in a couple of years. Really? Unless you've been in this situation you have no idea of what it's like, it wasn't suddenly going to be okay in two years' time, this was for life. Hearing his cynical words added to my misery and anger. I'd been assigned a social worker after my discharge but as I didn't know how to share how I was feeling inside, I fast learned that if I gave him the answers he wanted to hear and nod in the right places, he wouldn't hang around for long but leave me with a large pot of pills, my anti-depressants. I began to abuse these, in my reckless manner that I had come accustomed to. I took more than I'd been prescribed, washing them down with beer or vodka. They helped me to take the bitter edge off and aided the alcoholic dampening down of feelings. I became a class act at putting things mentally, 'in a box,' and pushing them away. There were those awful moments when I couldn't contain it any longer and it spurted out in massive emotional sobbing sessions. I'd completely lose it for that time and found it hard to stop crying, then it would gradually subside, I'd pull myself together and put the lid back on the box. It was nudging me all of the time, and I'd use the drink and prescription drugs to push it away temporarily. Fighting it was so hard, I'd never been in this dark place like this before. Sure, I'd experienced depressive feelings prior to my accident, but nothing like this. This was soul destroying. I hated myself, literally despised myself for everything I did and was. I disgusted myself for drinking whilst being a dad, hated myself for not being able to do things as I used to and I very much resented other couples still being together. They'd come to visit me, friends in couples, and I'd be secretly seething and feeling so bitter. How come they were happy and together? Why not me? It wasn't fair. I blamed everyone else but most of all, I blamed myself.

Then there was the shame I felt, and I became incredibly self-conscious. I'd go out with my friends, then quietly leave the local pub at 9.45pm before anyone else, and with a friend, we'd catch a taxi into town. Not wanting to be seen as different in any way, we'd arrive at the nightclub before anyone else so that I could get out of my chair and seat myself on a bench in the club. They hid my wheelchair behind the bar, and I'd make a start of drinking again before the crowds of partygoers would flock through the doors. For the next four hours I could pretend to be 'normal' again and blend into the crowd. I knew one of the bouncers well, Big George. He was an ex-Hell's Angel and as his name suggests, he was a hefty bloke. At the end of the night, once the club had cleared, George would heave my drunken body up and lift me back into my chair before I'd get a taxi home with a mate at my side. I was so ashamed of being different and drink helped me to feel that I could still be one of the lads and gave me a false sense of confidence. I'd think nothing of knocking back bottles of 20/20 and downing doubles and shots, crazily mixing my drinks all night. I actually got a few girlfriends as being that young lad, I received a lot of sympathy from females, and they'd come and talk to me. After a while, one of the girls I saw was the girl from the previous New Year's Eve. The one that Paula detested. She was still married to my friend but clearly not happy, just as Paula and I hadn't been. I had thought that there had been a spark at the time and I was right. Some of my mates knew that I'd started to see her, and it was an awkward situation to say the least. They were like piggy in the middle, mates with me but mates with the girl's husband too. I'd see her in the nightclub, then she'd come back to my flat before going home to her husband. I did feel guilty and knew it was wrong, this really wasn't my character. The next day, I'd block it out, blame everything on the drink as an excuse for my bad behaviour, this went on for a couple of months, sneaking about in a drunken state. Knowing that Paula hated her added to my passion and I was seeking revenge for what she had put me through.

After this one fizzled out to nothing, I almost immediately started another one again on another drunken night out, again with another friend's girlfriend. What was wrong with me?

12
Screwed Up

My life had changed dramatically and aside from my toilet habits, one of the other biggest shocks to the system had to be my sex life. This also did nothing for my self-esteem to the point that I had never returned to the unit for "the talk." It made me feel like a child and less of a man in all honesty. The girl I was seeing for these few months was actually the first person that I did sleep with after my accident. I say did, we tried, as although the area in my lower region could work, it would not work properly as it needed to. More than a little embarrassing.

It was around this time that on one of my regular nights out, I'd returned home alone and worse for wear with alcohol. I'd never done this before and I somehow managed to bump on the ramp going into my flat and fall out of my chair. I couldn't believe it and it soon sobered me up as I knew I needed help and was scared to death that I'd done some more damage. Not because I cared so much about my health at that stage but I did not want my life to be any more challenging than it already was. I pulled myself round as much as I could and shouted for help. After my initial examination, tests and further prodding in hospital, another major operation was on the cards for me. Thankfully my back was fine, no further damage caused but the surgeon did need to remove my metal rods. Coming round from the op, there was the usual grogginess after a general anaesthetic and I recognised the smiling faces of my family at my bedside. Surprisingly, instead of removing my back rods, the doctor had discovered that I needed more rods and screws inserting to support me. I was now, not dissimilar to a patchwork. Luckily for me you could not see any of the metal handiwork, it was all under my skin. I sometimes wondered what would have happened if you'd have put me too close to a metal detector. It wasn't long after this incident that my fling fizzled out.

Girls would notice me in my wheelchair and it seemed to draw some of them to me, along with my drink infused confidence. It brought out their empathic natures I suppose, which was a bonus for me at the time. On the outside looking in though, they would have no idea of the harsh reality of how hard my disability made it to have a relationship. If they wanted to get involved the realness of it was never long to rear its ugly head. I was totally screwed up on every level, physically, mentally, emotionally... a bloody mess. The hurt I felt was eating away at me in my sober moments, it drove me to want to seek revenge on the world. If I could be hurt this much, everyone else could be - I lost all morality about other people around me, the raging hurt took over me and controlled my decisions.

The partying lifestyle continued, in between my sober days of having the kids with me, those treasured times. Within a month of the other fling ending I was seeing another of my mate's girlfriends.

I was acting so out of character, even if she was also in an unhappy relationship, it was inexcusable. I only behaved like this when I was under the influence of alcohol and once I'd sobered up I was disgusted with myself for what I was doing and had morphed into. The self-loathing pushed me into drinking even more to excess and I was stuck in this vicious cycle with no idea of how to get out of it, and whether I actually cared enough to was more to the point. It was crazy, like most of the other actions I was taking, but this girl moved into my flat after just months of seeing one another. She split up with my mate but we didn't know what we were doing and clinging to each other in a warped sense of comfort. I still wanted my old lifestyle, I realised what a mistake moving in together had been and I had started to dabble in drug taking now as well.

The rave scene was starting to explode in the UK and with that came the drug, Ecstasy. It was an accepted part of a club night and most people were into popping the little tablets and then wildly dancing all night long. The high from the drug meant that a lot of clubbers only drank water whilst they raved in their vibrant club wear and made their moves on the dancefloors under the flashing of strobe lighting. It was first introduced to me in the club, I didn't take much encouraging from my friends to try it as the dark place I was in I had abandoned all thoughts of being sensible, health conscious or caring for anything. It turned out to be the best lift for me that I had found, much more effective than alcohol or prescribed drugs. The higher I became, the more normal I felt and to me that was simply amazing. I had forgotten what that felt like the past few months in this black tunnel I'd found myself in. The downside was, that as you came off of it, you could feel ten times worse. I timed it well though, I'd take it on Friday and Saturday nights after drinking all day, by Monday I'd feel rubbish but was perked up by Abbi being there and then I'd use anti-depressants to see me through to Thursday before the drinking kicked off again. As with any kind of addiction, you search hard and find a way to justify it to yourself. "You're not as bad as them Jace," I'd tell myself, half convinced as I wasn't downing the tablets every day like some people. I think some of the mental turmoil I was in was intensified by this conflict of trying to force my mind to believe I didn't have a problem. My subconscious knew that I was lying but the other part of my mind was doing its damnedest to persuade me otherwise. What a joke.

We started to go to the raves, and *Renaissance Club* in Derby was right in the heart of this trend. I loved the whole scene, music and all. My mates would start queuing to get access to the club, then once they let it be known they were with me, they'd get straight in. I became a focus of attention in many ways, and this time I didn't mind as I began to be accepted. The relief of feeling normal for those few hours out of a week was enormous for me. People, strangers even, loved me being there! They came from everywhere to speak to me, everyone high on this happy drug. They actually wanted to see the guy in the wheelchair. When I first arrived at the club I'd feel self-conscious and the first time I got out of my chair, as I'd done before, to sit on a seat, I was warned that wasn't a good idea as the club would get packed out, so I got back into my wheelchair. Sure enough, in no time, we were crammed in like sardines but the atmosphere was electric. I stayed in my chair. I felt self-conscious until the club filled up, as people would notice the difference between me and them, and then it was not a problem. I had my chair on a low podium which brought me to the same height as the rest of the room, fantastic. It was bizarre for me, with everyone frantically dancing around me, I got to dance in my chair. The buzz was incredible. The rave scene was just a move forward from the Northern Soul scene my brother and I had loved. I fondly remembered tales of his all-nighters when I was a young teen, although he never took drugs, I embraced it all. It was liberating to feel good and normal again, I'd be immersed in the whole experience, leave at 4am, catch up on a couple of hours sleep, then be driving.

The addiction for me was not about the drug, but about what it brought me, inclusion. Ecstasy took me on the journey from not caring about being alive to wanting to be. Anti-depressants or alcohol didn't have that power. When you have paralysis, that part of the body fights your blood pressure so I did myself no favours on this score. I became dehydrated after drinking all day, in order to have the confidence to go out in the first place, but even though I drank water in the club, I'd sweat profusely through the exercise that I wasn't used to and the body heat in the club. MDMA in it's true form was recommended in the 1950's to spice up flagging marriages, as it made couples love each other again. Similar to the enthusiasm of some religions, with their uplifting church ceremonies, all of the happy singing, clapping and dancing. These people would have an amazing week after lifting their spirits so high each Sunday. They'd get through each week, dipping as it gets nearer to the weekend before they have their fix all over again. They certainly notice it if they miss a week. I knew that my family suspected I was taking something and could not understand it for a moment, why would they? Nothing relieved the build-up of stress as this ritual did and it became my coping method for the next two years. I felt very guilty in between my highs and I knew my personality had been taken over as I fell out with my mum a lot, my moods were very erratic, more than ever.

The only stability in my life was my children, bless them both. Also financially I was stable. The severity of my disability warranted me to receive housing benefit, disability benefit and a car allowance. This helped me out a lot and was one less worry, but I had also started legal proceedings into a case of compensation for my accident, which seemed like it could be a long journey from what my solicitor advised. What was one more battle I thought? Because we were working on a building site of Islamic institute with no insurance (Paula's dad had no insurance), as times were tough, he was trying to get work for us, cutting corners, cutting costs and had the idea of getting it, compensation would be 50% at best, and legal aid was a lifesaver. We got a case going but it was one step forward, then more hurdles, so slow and very draining.

13
The Displeasures of The Flesh

That first Christmas of being stuck in my wheelchair was not the best. When I reminisced of the Christmas just 12 months before, that had seemed dreadful at the time, my marriage on the rocks, work scarce and the financial pressures that had seemed crippling. That now seemed no big deal on reflection, and how fortunate I actually had been with my full health, family around me and actually being able to go out and work. The fact that the work was scarce seemed irrelevant now, I didn't realise just how lucky I was to have legs that worked and allowed me to live the life I had. How easy it is to slide into that place of taking things for granted. Sadly, it's often only when you lose the most important things in your life, the "things" that actually really, truly count, that matter and make the difference, that we realise how fortunate we were all along. Wow, how so much had significantly changed in that time. It shocked me to my core when I took those still moments to reflect, I'd feel the tears well and I'd get that dark sinking feeling in my heart. Then my gut reaction was to push these emotions aside, bury them once more, push them down with vodka or drown them out with ecstasy.

Christmas day was spent at my parents. Mum was catering for us all and loved nothing more than having our little family together and us all celebrating in high spirits. My sister Sharon was going too, with her husband and their kids. Well, that's how the story used to go... I delighted in seeing Sam and Abbi in the morning for a short while. Seeing them excitedly tear open their pressies from Santa was a memory to treasure, these moments I lived for and kept me going. Feeling their little soft arms around my neck, feeling them plant their soppy kisses on my face and the word "Daddy," and "Santa," shrieked. Pure magic. I was saddened to see them then go back to their mum's for the day, but accepted we had to share the kids. Also, I was looking forward to seeing my mates at the pub for a Christmas day drink.

The pub opened its doors at midday and we all piled in. Everyone was in higher spirits than usual, all except me, or so it felt. I knew that once I'd got a few beers down my neck and some vodka chasers, I'd be ready to face the family at home. Mum had requested that I come home for 1pm, for dinner. Getting into the swing of things, and drinks a plenty I was not ready to leave at this time, I was only just warming up. Not long after this, my brother in law turned up. Mum had sent him to get me back home. I convinced him to stay for a drink, egged on by my mates too, and the boozing continued. By the time it hit 3pm, Sharon arrived, not looking very impressed and also cross with her husband for joining us. The Christmas dinner was getting spoilt and it was my fault. I reluctantly left with them both and we returned to mum's. I knew she would not be in a good mood, but neither was I. If I had it my way, Christmas would have been cancelled that year, there was nothing to bloody celebrate was there? We all sat around the table eating our starters, prawn cocktail, washed down with lager. My mind went to Sam and Abbi and wondered what they were doing right now? I felt a pang of hurt that they were not here.

"Jason, please can you leave the table love whilst I clear it for the turkey dinner?" A harmless request from mum, but for me, in that moment, it tipped me over the edge.

"Why should I move? Why me?" I reacted as though I was being picked on. She looked at me in shock, her face said it all. Where was the Jason that we know and love? I argued some more before wheeling myself in an angry huff through to the front room. Dad followed me, glaring and demanded to know why I'd spoken to mum like that and how ungrateful I was behaving. I blew up, my pent up rage exploding and before I knew it, I hurled a can of lager at him that I was drinking, the can hitting his arm and soaking him in beer. I stormed out, as fast as my chair could go, it's amazing how the passion of emotions can speed you up or slow you down. I went home in a foul mood and drank the minute I got back, attempting to block off what had just happened. Later on as I sobered up, I felt deeply guilty and the shame was eating away at me. How could I have behaved like that to my family? God, they must hate me for all I've put them through. Could I sink any lower if I tried? I was shocking myself, I never dreamed I'd be the person I'd become. I was despicable.

I spent the rest of Christmas Day at my sister's, feeling sheepish. A couple of days later, I saw my parents and apologised profusely for what I'd done, ruining the special day and being so nasty. They lovingly forgave me but I knew that they didn't understand how I felt. No-one did. The drink and drugs were distorting everything and I was living on a knife's edge most of the time, there was no end to it.

With the so-called festive season out of the way, I visited the unit to see my consultant and to partake in the "talk." I kind of geared myself up to it as I knew it would be cringeworthy, imagining myself in his office discussing the ins and outs of my sex life. Ugh. His first words were to tell me not to worry about it. Now that was easier said than done. I was excruciatingly embarrassed. I went into the curtained cubicle, stripped off and waited for him to come in. As the curtains moved, I saw a young female nurse appear. I felt my face redden instantly, feeling so vulnerable. As she began to explain the procedure, my cheeks burned furiously. Was she embarrassed as I was? Where was the doctor? I had to inject a drug into the side of my penis, it was known as penile injection therapy. As my spinal cords had damaged the area that is responsible for my being able to produce an erection, I was able to achieve it through this method and still have a sex life. There were four levels to using this substance however, and when it came to first testing it out, I was advised to try it in stages, starting with only injecting a quarter of the drug and seeing how my body responded. That was very important as if not used correctly, this chemical can cause a prolonged erection, priapism, and if this is left untreated, can be dangerous and result in penile tissue damage. Ouch. There were also possible side effects of bruising, scarring or infection. It did not sound very conducive to a romantic liaison. Then the major downside to this, I wasn't to drink alcohol at the same time as using it. It was enough to put me off trying.

When it came to putting this all into practice, I knew there was no way I'd be able to go through it without a few pints to relax me. I was so nervous at the thought of trying and if it didn't work and how humiliating that would be. Actually, how humiliating it would be anyway. With my situation as it was, the opportunity for sex was not so frequent, so on the evening I just thought I'd go all in and injected the whole lot of the drug. Completely ignoring the medical advice I'd received. I knew that if it didn't work that night, I'd have to wait until week to try, and it had taken a lot of courage to build myself up to this stage. It was instant, and certainly did the trick. I was so relieved. Several hours later, after the act itself, it was still there. They were not kidding. It panicked me as I recalled the serious side effects. Typical of my reckless mindset I suppose at the time. The following morning, the girl took me to casualty at the local hospital. Talk about embarrassing. She wheeled me in and I was wearing loose clothing with a tea-towel placed strategically across my thighs, creating a wigwam structure on my lap. The staff had to inject me to release my state. What an end to the performance, it felt theatrical, not the most natural experience to enjoy. It intensified my already self-consciousness, yes, physically it worked, but I had no feeling there and mentally it destroys you. I felt that I had to do it to prove myself as a man and to please my girlfriend. There were also the outside influences, with everyone judging me, wondering how I did it. Even my family and friends made the assumption that because a girl was with me, it had to be for my money or because they felt pity on me. That cut deep. Drugs helped me to cope with these feelings. It takes its toll on the partner as well, as it also makes them the centre of unwanted attention. Even though I was half pleased to have the opportunity to be sexually active again, it was a massive knock on my manhood. As a young guy, there was a lot of peer pressure plus the raging hormones running throughout your body. The focus was always on the physical act itself, as opposed to a loving, tender relationship.

14
The Downward Spiral

By the February, my relationship had broken down, not all that surprisingly and the girl moved out. I'd started to see someone else and was heavily invested in my drug and drink lifestyle over the long weekends. It was spiralling more out of control, as the nature of any addiction does. I gave up on trying to have any kind of a relationship as it just wasn't working.

The highlight of 1994 was that Abbi came to live with me full time. It was her choice and she still saw her mum alternate weekends and I still saw Sam. It gave me a new focus with Abbi with me all of the time. I secretly hoped that I'd be able to change my ways, but I felt too far sucked into the hell of addiction. It gave me the release that I craved and screamed out for, I could not give that up, how would I cope? When I was off of my head, it was the only time that I had an inkling of self-worth, and was accepted. That was a powerful pull and it enabled me to escape the realities of my life for short periods of time. It proved to be a very tough year. My football mates were anti-drugs and disapproved of what I was doing, so my friendships with that crowd waned and burnt out. That hurt as it wasn't such a black and white choice for me. Try living in this body I thought to myself, I couldn't help but feel bitter.

I had kept in touch with Sharman from *Lodge Moore* and she invited me back as it was closing down and they were holding a ceremony to mark the occasion. I did want to go as they had helped me a lot in that place and thought it would be good to see some familiar faces. The night before I had been out, had no sleep and was still feeling drugged up. A few days later, she rang me up and asked what I was doing? She had noted my pupils and my whole appearance and behaviour was a giveaway to a trained eye. I denied it and felt like a rabbit caught in the headlights. She was actually the first person to confront me, and although I was annoyed, I knew that she cared and I felt that.

The trouble with taking ecstasy were the hideous comedowns. After feeling elated and normal for several hours on my nights out, crashing back down to the misery of reality took its toll on me. To combat this, I began to abuse anti-depressants mixed with the alcohol. I was behaving as a seasoned drug taker but was actually a habitual user. It was not always guaranteed that you would get your hit though, which kind of added to the anticipation and the crazy risk taking mindset I was in. If I didn't get the drug I'd be devastated but still loved the thrill of not knowing. I felt part of an elite crowd, not dissimilar to how I felt in my mod days, as one of the cool crowd. I never, ever had drugs in the house. I drew the line at that. I began to feel the long term physical effects of taking drugs and the drink/drug lifestyle I was living. I'd be sleeping all day when Abbi was at school, eating rubbish, be out at night as much as I could, then partying afterwards back at mine with a crowd of mates, music blaring, going to bed drunk, all kinds of people staying over. This regular habit encouraged my upstairs neighbours to complain and bang on the ceiling, it didn't deter me. I was awful and merged into the antisocial version of me. I was two separate identities, the regular Jason, the dad that cared and the bad Jason who was on the path of self-destruction. All in all, I allowed it to happen, the drink and drugs I masked as my excuse but ultimately it was down to my decision. It was the only coping strategy I had. My neighbours also demonstrated compassion to the point of making allowances for my behaviour the following day. They knew of my daily struggles but their forgiveness made me worse as I felt I could get away with it.

Our crowd always went to the same nightclubs which suited me as I knew what to expect and how accessible they were. It was safe. There was someone's 21st birthday coming up and they were celebrating at a club in Sheffield. The DJ, Jeremy Healy was playing and although I did not want to miss out, I was reluctant to go, with self-doubts creeping in and I lost my confidence with it being a new place. I decided not to go. Instead I went out to the pub all day and drank masses, partly feeling sorry for myself as everyone else would be partying that night elsewhere. It highlighted my difference which was always distressing. Extra vodka sorted that out.

I was going back to the taxi rank on my own, worse for wear, when I bumped into some people that were going to the party. Everyone was getting there on a bus and they urged me to join them. Feeling secretly pleased and wanted, I relented and agreed to join them. I went home first though to freshen up after being out all day. A quick shower and a change of clothes and I was good to go. I had help to lift me onto the bus and felt the buzz of excitement of anticipation of the partying ahead of me, tinged with some anxiety of the unknown. My mouth was as dry as a bone and my head was mildly aching and slightly dizzy. I must have gotten dehydrated throughout the day's boozing and made a mental note to drink some water in the club. I knew that being in my chair and not moving, could amplify the symptoms and I could go downhill faster than others that had been drinking. This didn't stop me from buying three e's at the club and a bag of speed. The speed was to pick me up after the clubbing so I could carry on at the afterparty. I had it all planned out, being a seasoned drug taker now, I knew how to work it. Ecstasy was not a cheap habit, £12.50 for the tablets was the norm. Some had come onto the market apparently for £8 which I was offered that night. Delighted at the price reduction but at the back of my mind I had a niggle. Would it be okay? What the hell I thought, in my usual could not care less manner, swallowing the first one. The night began, it was an amazing club and as ever, the atmosphere was electric. Thirty minutes later, it all began to change. Whatever I had taken was having an adverse effect on me now, as I began to hallucinate for the first time ever. It was really scary as images loomed all around me in the club, all the faces looked evil staring at me and through the thudding music, flashing lights and smoke, I freaked out. I was struggling to distinguish what was real and what was not. I could make out that everyone else was having these weird experiences too, and were not in a position to help me. It got really bad as the hallucinations became more vivid, I don't know how I held it together until the end but I couldn't leave on my own. By the time I got back onto the bus back, my mates had settled down but I was getting worse and worse. It was terrifying and all I could see was blood and violence – the bus driver was trying to attack me and everyone else was out to stab me. I was screaming and thought my life was in serious danger. As I saw a sharp blade edging towards me and an evil man wielding the knife, it suddenly disappeared as I blacked out.

My friends panicked a bit as I fell into an unconscious slump but assumed I'd just taken a bad pill as they had. They hauled me off of the bus and rushed me off to Newark Hospital. By this time, dawn was almost starting to break through as they handed me to a nurse in the A&E department and left.

I was seen immediately and staff were concerned as my state rapidly worsened. My parents were contacted and rushed in and they rang around my mates to find out what I had taken. One of them told my dad. By this time, the staff knew the severity of my condition as my organs began to shut down. I was rushed off to Queen's Medical Centre as they were better equipped to deal with emergencies such as this. I was burning up and my body could no longer control my temperature and the medics had to induce a coma to give my body a fighting chance to recover. My parents were warned that it didn't look good as my organs continued to fail. They were distraught. I was placed on a special bed that maintained my body at the lowest temperature as possible. I was struggling to breathe so a tracheotomy was performed on my windpipe.

My parents stayed at my bedside religiously, worried sick that they were going to lose me. On day 15, the doctors gave up. They thought I had serious brain damage, my organs were still failing and they wanted to transfer me to Birmingham Hospital to have a kidney transplant as a last resort. It was an early case of ecstasy, nothing was working and they were frantically trying everything to save my life.

15
Coma

My dad said that he knew that I wouldn't survive if they moved me, and refused to let them switch off the life support machine. My dehydrated state had made the situation far worse. "My son is a fighter, and he'll fight to the end."

Dad had sat and held my hand, talking to me and sitting with me all night, every night, it had become a nightly vigil. Mum had been there with him, and my friend Tim had turned up at all obscure hours with flasks of soup for them and to check on me. He was a Godsend and a rock for my parents.

All of a sudden, the specialists had found a drug they wanted to try on me from St Thomas Hospital in London. There was hope again and my parents clung to each other, begging God to make it work for me and bring their son back. On day 17, I opened my eyes. My parents were there, waiting for me, and alerted staff in their thrilled state to see me conscious again. The relief they felt to have me back and they sobbed their hearts out in their exhausted state. I was not out of the woods though and was in a dreadful way. I was hallucinating heavily, worse than before my coma, drifting in and out of consciousness. Apparently, it's a fact that most people that have been in intensive care follow on with a psychotic episode. The hallucinations were mainly of a violent and very distressing nature. Each time my dad went out to fetch a coffee I would see him being aggressively attacked on the other side of the door, I saw hospital walls that oozed with blood and everyone was out to harm me. I was totally paranoid.

In my lucid moments I was very conscious that I had gone from being a patient that was cared for as a paraplegic, to being labelled by some staff as a drug taker and they had little empathy towards me. I felt racked with guilt. I couldn't speak for a few days, as each time the nurses tried to remove my tracheotomy my blood pressure shot up. They didn't know how to deal with it. By chance, Dr Winston was on a secondment at Queen's and he came to see me one day. He managed to take it out successfully and it was a relief to have my voice back, albeit very throaty to start with. I felt as though I had gravel in my vocal chords and the whole area was chronically sore. I felt battered as though I'd had a ten ton truck run me over. My family brought some paintings in that my kids had made me, and during my hallucinations, even they appeared distorted and I refused to believe that my kids had painted them. I dreaded the nights as I was convinced that the night staff were out to kill me. They were planning to harvest my organs to donate to other patients, each night they'd take me down to the hospital's dark basement where there was a circular saw hidden. I'd be screaming my head off as they dragged me towards it, knowing my legs were about to be chopped off and then believing they had as I couldn't feel my limbs. As if that wasn't disturbing enough, each night, three lads would come to my bed and start tampering with the machinery that surrounded my bedside. They'd inject poison into my bag and fiddle with my heart monitor, it was terrifying as I felt my life was being threatened and no-one stopped them.

One day I woke up on the ward and it was snowing everywhere. There was enough snow on the ward to build a snowman with and I began to believe it was bloody Christmas. When the psychosis finally subsided, and I heard all about my wild behaviour and delusions I struggled to believe it. I could vividly remember the threatening images in my mind but at the same time it was surreal. I'd had fluid on my lungs and a male nurse had drained them every hour and he'd been a little rough in how he handled me because he saw me as a druggie. The psychological effects were incredibly disturbing. I struggled to sleep for a long time afterwards as each night I had the vivid images stuck inside my head on replay, as though it were a stuck film reel. Most peculiar.

Even though I was out of the imminent danger zone with my health that I'd been in, I was shockingly in a worse condition than when I had first had my accident. I'd lost all of the sensation down one side, the muscle tone had gone, I could not put my hands up - leaving me quadriplegic. I was not able to speak either at first and faced another five months of recovery in hospital. I had to relearn how to dress myself, shower myself and other basic activities, I had to start all over again. I felt a million times worse because now many people were judging me, with the view that it was a self-induced state from my drug taking. Lots of the care vanished from others and it was a very gruelling time for me. I'd had a level of brain injury, and not sure of where to place me, the medics admitted me to a stroke ward. In effect, my injuries were very similar as the same part of my brain had been affected. It was dreadful and I was my biggest critic, comparing myself to the other patients, feeling guilty because I had caused my new condition myself. Even though it had been done out of desperation, I felt bad. My memory was shocking, I'd tell someone a story and two seconds later I'd have forgotten and would end up repeating myself. I was informed that my short term memory was gone and that no one else should attempt to correct me as it would increase my self-consciousness and I also had a very noticeable slur which only added to that. The prognosis was similar to a stroke and even after five months of being in hospital, it was going to take me longer to get back to the fitness level I'd previously had. It was a long slow process to build up all of the muscles on the side I had weakened, I was still very weak. I had to transfer from side to side now, so back at home, I had to have the flat readapted to suit me.

This was the big wake up call for me, I knew that I had to take a difference approach and do something different. I had no idea what though, except that I must change.

16
Something Had To Change

The flat was adapted to suit my latest health needs and at the same time I finally accepted that my self-destructive behaviour really was not doing me any favours. My mindset had to change as well, I could not continue as I was for any longer. My life was far from perfect but I did hold the desire to carry on, and David, the social worker I'd seen after leaving rehab came to visit me again in June 1995. He was also a counsellor and I agreed to try again, but this time I was to tell the truth so that he could actually have a chance to help me. He knew that our prior conversations had been rushed and that I had not been prepared to open up at that time. We went right back to the very beginning, exploring everything and talking it through. It was not an easy journey but I now realised a necessary one. To sort myself out, I had to look at the painful roots rather than to keep taking the sticking plaster approach of sharing surface feelings only and then blotting them out with substances or other external stuff.

I still drank, I'd have a couple of pints but it would soon feel like I was regressing back to like when I was on drugs again, alcohol clearly did not mix well with my brain injury. My GP actually said that I could never drink again, as I'd damaged the part of my brain that was susceptible to stimulant. This plunged me to a very low morale and began to take anti-depressants again. What with this and the counselling, it had to be a step in the right direction.

As I opened up to David over the forthcoming months, he was able to build up a picture of my past and everything that had led up to my current day circumstances. I was also reading some self-help books on my mission to change my thinking and find a way to be. As I dived into books about Buddhism, I discovered that elements of it offered me some comfort and useful techniques that I was able to implement. I adapted some of them to suit me but the main thing was that they helped me rather than reverting back to my old self destructive ways. One of the little strategies I used a lot of the time was using a scale to measure my mood. At one end was zero which stood for feeling suicidal and a ten would be to feel amazing. Wherever you were on the scale, each number had an opposite. A two is an eight, a three is a seven, a four is a six... When we reached five I questioned David over it. What would the opposite be, as there wasn't one? What I took from that was that I was not to go any further and get happy, as if I could be happy at a seven then I had to accept that I'd be experiencing a three also at some point. By remaining at number five it meant to me that I was neither happy nor sad, and five seemed a place that I could function from and cope day to day with the kids, without the use of drugs and heavy alcoholic intake. Once I started this, I used it for years as a coping mechanism. It may not have been the best solution but it worked for me. When I went to a wedding for example, I'd consciously ensure that I would not get too happy and automatically pull myself back and keep myself in check. This turned out to be the essence of what resilience actually is. I took from Buddhism what I needed to in my search for inner peace.

I had been called in for a six-month hospital outpatient appointment at The QMC Hospital in Nottingham to check up on my progress. The doctor seemed impressed with me, I had regained a lot of strength in my arms and I was now able to use all of my muscles groups and was not suffering the complications of full movement like a quadriplegic anymore. My speech had dramatically improved and my slur a lot less noticeable. The doctor was so impressed with my progress he said he could see no reason I wouldn't be walking again in 6 months. Wow, that really would be a miracle as I couldn't walk before! Embarrassed the doctor realised, and I laughed saying there was no need to apologise, at least the whole incident had not affected my humour.

In the September of that year, after a few months of counselling, I came across another positive interest that would allow me to help myself, plus it looked great fun! I saw the television advert for water skiing for people with disabilities and knew I had to try it out. It was the end of the season but I tested it out one weekend and found that I loved it. It took me away from everything, the daily struggles and was a very refreshing escape that would not harm me. I decided that I'd take it up regularly the next season.

I was still going out socially with my mates but had to monitor how much I drank. They became more like my carers than my friends now, as I'd feel drunk after just a couple of pints, that didn't change. When I got tired, the slur would return, not as obviously but noticeably so. I learnt to line my stomach well with a good meal before going out to the pub.

My battle with my compensation case looked set to be a long drawn out saga. Since the initial visit with a solicitor after I was approached in hospital, it had been explained to me just how complex my case was, due to the circumstances and it involving an Islamic school. At the back of my mind, I always thought this would be the light at the end of the dark tunnel, the money would help to set me up, make everything better, buy a house and offer me security.

The following water-skiing season began, so there I was all ready to get stuck in at *Holme Pierrepont* in Nottingham. It was a large country park with a big expanse of water and they offered many different water sport activities. The group I was a part of was organised by an amazing charity, the British Disabled Water Skiing Association, and each one of us had a disability of some sort, blindness, amputees, you name it - they were a great crowd with real positive spirit. I took to going monthly and the kids were a part of it too. It was a great experience for them to be around others with disabilities and witness their struggles but also their incredible determination. It was very humbling. We formed some solid friendships and it felt like a family unit, all looking out for one another. I felt understood and accepted by this supportive network of people who got me, I no longer felt like a freak. That really helped my confidence and self-esteem. The kids loved it too, making friend with everyone. Abbi used to borrow Tracey's crutches, pretending she was disabled and hobble about. I can remember once that Sam had gone missing with another youngster, Ryan. We knew that they hadn't gone far and when we found them they appeared a little sheepish and a bit quiet which was most unusual for them. It was then, that we discovered that they had both suffered an electric shock from the fencing that portioned off the horses in the field. Each year we'd have a camp, which was always fun, and everyone involved their families too, if they had them. It was a challenge to start with and took me a while to gain the skills I needed, but through persistence I became pretty good. It was the answer for me at that time in my life

I would be at *Holme Pierrepont* once a month, have the kids and the other weekends where I had nothing to do, I'd go out for a few drinks. I was consciously trying to make things right as I recognised the damage I had done to those around me by not coping. This became my new and regular routine.

By 1998 the Islamic trust made me an offer of £400,000, half the value of the case, for me to go away and the case to be finished. I was advised to accept as my case was so complex. It was short lived as the offer shouldn't have been made, then I was informed that there were many issues left to solve but the offer had been made now, so at least that was still on the table. The case continued, with endless meetings with solicitors, the money was going to be my saviour eventually but added to my stress load considerably. Why did it all have to be so hard?

I started watching Nottingham Forest again in 1998 with my great friend Moley, after saying that I'd never watch a match again, in a chair. He had suffered with health problems for years, with stunted growth which had meant years of operations for him. Yet he always made the most of his life, he never once complained and he was a huge influence on me. He said to me one day, "I've had years of this, this is how it is and you've got to get on with it." It really made me rethink things as everyone looked up to him after what he'd been through.

In 2000 Sam came to live with me, Abbi was already with me fulltime. Their mum had started a family with her partner and had two other kids by this point and I think that Sam began to feel a little pushed out. He was now 8 years old and full of life and adventurous - he stole matches from the cupboard, got a can of deodorant and singed all of his face, a typical lad. After breakfast he'd go out and play with his mates, the street was really safe, a cul-de-sac, just like when I was a child, always playing in someone's garden. I thought this was my answer now, I had the kids, I could bring them up as I wanted to. Watching my dad kick a ball around the garden - how had I not thought of this before? It dawned on me that I was never going to play football with my boy. It was heart breaking. A positive for me though was that I was able to convert him from being a Manchester United Fan and instil the misery of becoming a long suffering Forest fan. It was all about them, they were my everything, and this became another way of coping as I put all of my focus onto them. I got to be the dad that most are not privileged to be, taking them to and from school each day, going to see their plays at school. It was a blessing to be able to do this for them. There were advantages to my situation after all.

During the times when I wasn't skiing, or with the kids, or out drinking with my mates, my darkness would creep back in. Even with the work I had done on myself. When issues still have not been dealt with, they surface again and again until you either face them head on and heal or they persist. My deeper struggles were so very painful, fears of being rejected again were prominent for me, of feeling unwanted, unloved. I slowly started to drink more again, it was a subtle change and no-one noticed to start with, or they didn't say anything. It certainly wasn't as major as before but the aim was to get drunk and forget. I felt my sadness within and I couldn't handle it. Obviously, the kids were with me all of the time now, but my mum helped me out a lot when dad was working away. I guess we helped one another, as she'd feel lonely whilst dad wasn't there. I'd just go out one night a week for my release and by sticking with that I coped, this quickly turned into two nights. I had come a long way forward in the last few years since my fall, when I stopped to reflect. It's as though I still had this chunk of sadness stuck inside of me, some of it had shifted but some of it lingered.

I'd made a great friend in Pete, from water skiing, in fact several good friends from that crowd. They were pretty amazing. Pete had rented a place out in Tenerife and he began to invite me and the kids out with him for a couple of weeks, he'd stay for three months at a time. I can't blame him, the weather was terrific and it was his escape no doubt.

When Abbi was 15 we started to have a few more petty arguments, she was the only girl in the house but she had also got that awkward stage in her life and maybe I wasn't as supportive as I could have been. Also at this time Sam was 13 and the house wasn't quite as happy as it had been when they were younger. Abbi started staying at friend's houses at the weekends and now admits to attending a few parties as teenagers do and she thought she may have an easier time if she went to live with her mum. I was heartbroken, she had been such a lovely daughter, always exceeding at school and I didn't want her to go, but instead of trying to convince her to stay and offering more support and a little more flexibility now she was older, to help her get through this teenage angst, I gave her an ultimatum, "you're free to choose where you live but if you go you can't come back." Maddened by what I had said she packed a bag and went to her mums. On reflection after all had calmed down I thought maybe living with her mum at this awkward time of her life might be what she needed and we soon picked up our usual loving relationship. I knew I had to let her go and she would be ok, she initially struggled, not getting the GCSE's she was capable of but enough for sixth form but she left in the first year. She enrolled at college and worked part time in various jobs before meeting Fergus and her life quickly settled down again and she landed a job at Barclays bank.

17
The Pub Years

The ethos of the water skiing charity was that you learnt to ski and then moved on. I think there is a lesson in there that we could all gain something from.

After much practice over the months of spending time with the crowd at Nottingham, I became proficient and my intention was to get onto the water ski team to compete. In 1999 I began to train up in Whitworth in Lancashire at the ski centre there ran by Great Britain coach Andy Knowles and his wife Flo. For the first season, me and the kids camped in the dormitory, staying overnight for the weekends. We'd cook for ourselves in the dorm and after getting to know Andy and Flo, we'd invite them down to join us for something to eat. They lived on the premises upstairs in their own quarters. The social occasion included a couple of beers, naturally, with me still trying to escape. I trained there for four years, my skills grew as I was able to branch out into performing tricks, jumps and slalom, which entailed me weaving in and out of water buoys, all were tricky at first but the focus to improve was brilliant for me. I experienced a sense of freedom on the water, I was me again, free of being stuck in my wheelchair, my legs may not have worked anymore but I could do this! I made some other friends, including Ellie, a young girl that had lost both of her legs. Over time, the socialising seemed to take over and we would all drink into the early hours. One thing became clear to me, and that was most people that I came across who also had a severe disability also turned to drink, drugs or both in order to cope with their feelings. I certainly was not on my own with this. My regret is that although I was improving I was not fulfilling my potential. I didn't quite make the team as I was too focussed on the knocking back beers in the evenings which meant that I didn't get out as early the following morning and be on the water putting in the practice. I did not make the grade which I was disappointed about, but knew it was my own fault, well the drunken personality I had at least, as the sober Jason wouldn't have done this. Once in those circles it was hard to recognise when unhelpful habits were creeping back in, everyone would be in a team spirit, jollying one another along fuelled with alcohol. So by trying to escape the drinking culture back home, I just ended up in a similar scene just in a different town.

Back in Farndon and at my local, *The Rose and Crown*, the landlords would change hands over the years. They all knew me well and it was an incredibly supportive extended family for me, everyone looking out for me. I was in an okay place, coping from one week to the next, the drug taking behind me, but I was far from thriving.

It was a couple called Nip and Moira running the pub when I first had my accident. Lovely couple, salt of the earth, and they put up with my drunken episodes. Looking back, I must have been a nightmare customer, as once I'd had a few drinks, I'd change character completely and become this larger than life bloke doing some outrageous antics, entertaining everyone for a laugh. I loved that, a bit like when I'd been at school - adopting the class clown façade. I'd be forever falling out of my chair as the drinking would get out of hand, in the end, the ambulance staff got to know me and we were on first name terms. The amount of minor injuries I'd have, black eyes, cuts, bruises, you name it, I did it to myself. After a particularly lively night, I'd pop back to the pub the next day to make my blushing apologies to Nip and Moira. It would always be laughed off, but I felt a guilty fool.

Joe and Linda were the next landlords - we did have some laughs as they started to organise pub trips abroad. A whole load of us would pile onto a coach and off we'd go, lots of merry making on the way. I refused to go on the trips at first, but the water skiing had increased my self-confidence and I had the attitude of, "sod it, I'm going," else I would have missed out on some great fun times.

One trip to Belgium will go down in history as one of the biggest screams. From the coach, we all caught the overnight Ferry to Ostend on our way to Brussels. There was no going to bed early, or even at a reasonable time for us, as we took full advantage of the ferry's disco and bar. I was especially over the top that night, and fell out of my wheelchair seven times! Yes seven times, you can imagine the bruises. I think the wear and tear on my poor wheelchair took its toll, as after the seventh time of tipping over and landing on the sticky dancefloor, one of the wheels collapsed as several spokes snapped, causing the wheel to hurtling me out of the chair and the wheel itself spun across the floor whereas my mates were dancing to the poppy tunes of Abba. No-one could believe it and amidst giggles and drunken snorts, I was picked up and carried to my cabin. I was so drunk I didn't notice the rocky sea that night and just collapsed fast asleep on my bed. On awaking the next morning, I thought I'd dreamed the whole fiasco, then as I opened my bleary eyes I spotted the bashed up chair crumpled up in the corner by the door. Good grief, it had actually happened. Now what, I had no bloody chair! My mates had a scour around the ship decks and managed to find a great big heavy old-fashioned wheelchair, it reminded me of the models in the rehab ward that we had all hated and dreaded using. They borrowed it and brought it to me and I got myself up and ready and met everyone in the dining hall. After a hearty breakfast and several cups of tea, we may have felt better but we'd overslept and were now disembarking. As I was pushed off of the ferry to meet the coach, as it was not one you could self-propel, the first stop was to see if we could find me a wheel replacement for my own chair. Not likely in this foreign city as they were not exactly a convenience store item you found on most corners. There we were about six of us, trekking into Brussels on a wheelchair mission. We must have looked a sight, God knows what the Belgian's thought... After pacing a few streets, we turned a corner and randomly there stood a wheelchair store across the street. After a half an hour exchange of poor French, lots of pointing and ums and ahs, we came away with a shiny new wheel that fitted like a glove. That experience did nothing but to add to my drunken, and always ready for a laugh Jason reputation!

Then there was Jeff and Marie, this couple encouraged me to host the Sunday Quiz Night. I'd get blind drunk, roll out a funny quiz but by the time it came round to dish out the answers, I'd have drank even more and struggled to read them out to the pub crowd. It was the same with karaoke. I'd sit quietly in a corner when I was sober, but put a few drinks inside me and you wouldn't get me off of the mic all night.

We used to have lock-ins at the pub, staying there until about 2-3am and I reached the point where I'd sometimes go home on my own. I had my own little route mapped out as directly as possible to my flat, but there was an area I named the black spot. At this point there was a bit of a kerb and if I was to fall out anywhere it was always bang on this spot, without fail. On this night, it was the early hours by the time I'd got home, but after rummaging around for my front door key, it was nowhere to be found. I got myself into a flap and in an agitated state, rang the pub to ask them if my key was there. It had to be. Whilst they turned the pub upside down, searching high and low, I made my way back, whilst someone else was sent out to retrace my steps whilst foraging around in the pitch black with a torch. I was rather grumpy by the time I arrived at *The Rose and Crown* and looked in dismay when they said my key had not been found. However, a moment or two later, Marie suggested that I look on my belly. As I peered down, I saw the edge of the metal key protruding out where it was lodged on my stomach fold. Two hours of key hunting and it was on me all that time! So for years to come, I became the running joke anytime anything went astray, "check under Jace's belly," they'd all joke. *The Fjellgar* was another great pub I would spend a lot of time in run by Kev and Jenny, it was a converted Norwegian barge moored in the marina in the village, they too encouraged me to host the Sunday quiz for them, again I would always be slightly tipsy when it came to giving out the answers.

Colin and I spent a lot of time going out together in the 00's, often ending up in unplanned situations. After one heavy session in town we were dropped off in the village at 3am, it was during the winter and was a cold foggy night. I subsequently fell out of my chair, like I did. Colin tripped over his own feet and we both just lay there, on the cold hard ground, too drunk to fathom out our next move. Through the fog, appeared a face we knew and loved, it was Moley! He'd clearly been on his way home from a Rose and Crown lock-in, and without uttering a word, he did nothing more than to pick me up, place me back in my chair and disappeared back into the fog. He was a strong chap. It struck us as rather comical in that moment. The next morning, I woke up and told Colin, who had stayed over, about my dream. He chuckled when he said it was no dream, it had really happened. No wonder I was forever finding bruises and not sure where they came from. Moley loved his trips to Thailand, and he'd always say to me that he didn't want me to become too reliant on him as he might not always be around. He wasn't wrong, as sadly he suffered a heart attack in 2004. It was a huge shock, he was such a rock to me and it left a big gap for quite some time.

Heavy fog, nights out and wheelchairs do not mix well. As after another night's lock-in, on the way home with Niall this time, the fog was low lying at waist height which was rather eerie. I did nothing more than to fall out of my chair again, followed by Niall tripping over me, the effects of too much beer and his reflex actions impaired. There we were, both lying in the road, the fog swirling above us, when a neighbour's car drove down the street. Luckily for us my feet were just sticking above the fog line, my six foot height saved us that night. Niall had a large family headed up by John and Pam, they became like my second family, and there was always a McGuiness or two where ever we went. If for some reason there wasn't a late drink at *The Rose*, we would head to the *Caledonian*, the name we had for John and Pam's back garden. John heralded from Glasgow and he always had a healthy supply of beer in the outhouse. We would try really hard to be quiet but the noise of 10-15 people in their back garden would inevitably wake them up. John would come down stairs, but not to find out what the hell was going on, but to join us for a drink, we had some great times in the *Caledonian*. John was stalwart of the village and his passing in late 2015 was a great loss and Pam sadly passed a year later. The *Caledonian* though still continues, as Niall's sister Fiona now lives there.

I was always grateful for the support my mates gave me over the years, but I had to sometimes enforce some boundaries. The night that springs to mind was when Stewart and I had been out, obviously worse for wear we came back to mine, chatting and laughing. The next thing I knew was that he began to strip off his clothes and was just about to climb into my bed. I asked him what on earth he was doing and with no further ado told him he was sleeping in the spare bed, pointing firmly in the direction of the spare room. My friends had got so used to supporting me, like a cross between great mates and carers, but sharing my bed was not one of the caring acts I was about to gratefully receive...

Sometimes our drunken antics would take us further afield, and on this occasion it was to Whitley Bay, the Las Vegas of the UK for Dave's stag-do. My self-doubts and insecurities flooded in as it was going to be somewhere new and I had to stop in a different hotel to most of the gang as it wasn't accessible for me, but I knew I'd have a great support with me and decided to go. The night ended up at a lap dancing club and Dave was treated to his own private show. The only problem was, this private dance was right at the top of the building and there was no lift. There was nothing else for it, but they all formed a team and carried me in my chair right up the flights of stairs, bearing in mind they were all well-oiled at this stage. A few hours later, after much laughter, more beer and some ogling at naked flesh we got ready to leave. Now all in a much more inebriated state, we pondered over how on earth were we going to get me down all of the flights of stairs and back to the hotel? Joe, who was a burly chap, took charge of the situation and helped me, then tripped and fell head over heels down the steps, followed by me in the chair. You can imagine the sights and sounds we made. God knows how, but I remained intact and in my chair, meanwhile Joe was flat out dazed and sprawled on the floor. Alerted by the mass noise we made, all of the scantily clad girls in the bar ran out, saw the collision and asked if I was okay? Joe got no sympathy whatsoever. Being in a chair is hard, but you do get a lot of attention and empathy from folks.

Lifts made life much easier for me as you can imagine, however it depends entirely on who you are in the lift with and in this case it was Stewart. After enquiring if I'd ever jumped up in a lift whilst it was going down, to create the experience of feeling like a spaceman floating, I replied that I hadn't. The next minute, he jumped into a full on demonstration, doing no more than stopping the lift in its tracks, shutting it down and us getting stuck. Just as well we had no phobias of small spaces, or of stuck elevators between us. Having no choice but to use the emergency phone to ring for help, we soon heard the fire engine sirens in the distance. A couple of minutes later, an axe came through the lifts doors prising it open. On seeing my chair, they then had to wind the lift back up from the shaft so that I could wheel myself out. The embarrassment we felt was to another level so we used false names, just as well as only a few days later, a Mr. Black and a Mr. Smith featured in a local newspaper article.

Before all of these nights out I'd usually go to mum's for tea on a Saturday. Mum was a smashing cook and it was her way of looking after me, to feed me up before a night out and afterwards the next day, for Sunday lunch. It was always at 1pm on the dot, the great Sunday roast. Sometimes I wouldn't have got to bed until the early hours and would still be drunk and have to force my meal down, as if I didn't clear my plate, she'd want to know what was wrong. I knew that I'd hurt them so much in the past. She would worry if I drank but also worry if I didn't go out.

Throughout this period there always seemed to be someone that I'd have a drunken casual fling with, but it was never more than that for me. I'd be drunk in the pub or club and by the end of the night I knew I'd be going home with them. I craved the attention and to feel normal, but it never felt real. Behind all of this charade was the ultimate fear of rejection. People would see the wheelchair, they would accept it, but then they'd find out about all of the other stuff that came with it. It was easier to keep people at arm's length because if I couldn't live with it, how the hell would someone else?

Despite the fun times and laughter, it may sound as though I was turning my life around, but I wasn't. I was simply masking everything.

18
The Bounce?

All of those people around me kept me going through thick and thin. Pete became a great friend and my reference point. He'd been in his chair for 15 years longer than me, so he gave me lots of great advice and I'd run things by him. We had many more trips out to Tenerife, not just for weeks, but for longer periods of time in the sunshine. Sometimes, Andy and Flo would bring Sam and Abbi out to join me, when I'd gone out in school time. The partying would continue over there, with regular boozy nights out.

I enjoyed spending time with people who lifted me up and who listened and didn't judge me. Lisa, Paula's sister was one of these. I think my family were a bit suspicious at the time, querying why I was still friends with her when I had nothing to do with my ex-wife? She became a great confidante and whatever I shared with her would go no further and we'd have nights out too.

My own family were superstars. Sharon was a constant support, always there for me whenever I needed her. My parents helped out in many ways. Financially, constantly helping me out, taking the kids on holiday abroad, practically, they'd take care of the gardening and some of the house chores, I know that I wasn't always as appreciative as I could have been. I guess you always take it out more on your nearest and dearest. Sarah, my lovely cousin, was married but she always made time for me and the kids. We'd spend weekends at hers, I'd kip on the settee and she'd make a fuss of Abbi and Sam, always protective of us all.

I kept in touch with Tim, my friend from my sign writing job days and ever since the accident he was there for me, often taking me on hospital runs to my appointments, and there were many over the years. He always found time for me and my problems. I probably never really appreciated all he did for me enough. Even when he was in a relationship with Alie, he always made sure I was okay and I would spend many nights sleeping over at theirs after one party or another. I was very fortunate I had him as a friend. Although I don't see Tim these days I will always be extremely grateful for what he did for me over the years.

It was heart-warming to have this incredible supportive network, my family, and friends from all of the different parts of my life, all coming together to help me. It demonstrates how we are all connected really. Human connection, essential for us to thrive and not just survive.

The legal wrangle continued, I'd lost count of the hours I'd spent in the solicitor's office and because it had been such a drawn-out complex case, my legal representative had changed a few times. By 2004 the consensus was that land value had gone up in price massively so my options were to either go after this offer or go back to court. If I rejected the offer and return to court then I ran the risk of receiving nothing. A few months later, during 2005 we went to court. I'd had enough of waiting, it had been twelve years since the proceedings had begun. We had pushed and pushed, I was tired and wanted an outcome. I hired a legal team of a Barrister and a Judge and we entered into the Royal Courts of Justice. The last twelve years of stress were about to come to an end in this room, I longed for the release. Judge, His Honour English Jones's court was in Buckingham Palace, the Judge at my hearing bowed to him as he was so highly ranked, whilst my opponents had only a barrister to represent their side. Almost straight away they agreed to paying their offer, the relief was tremendous. The Judge stood up and announced that the court to be adjourned. Two hours later, we were back in the courtroom. We agreed to accept the £400,000. I had hoped this to be the ending as it was a perpetual reminder of my past and of the struggle. Alas, this was not to be the case. Out of court they wouldn't pay up and in these circumstances it then becomes a civil debt. Unbelievably, you have to then follow further procedures and take them back to court. For reference's sake, this is the longer version for my book. On their refusal to pay, I had a meeting with my solicitor and he explained my two options. I already had an agreement signed by them for the £400,000 but I could choose to turn that into a debt which we could then chase them for and for each day they do not pay we could charge them interest, forcing them to pay. I chose this latter option. It took us another two years with the sum finally at £408,000, by this stage I had employed three solicitors because they had each been promoted throughout the duration of my case. They stated that they had never had a case like it before and it made history becoming a case law. This created a reference point for future similar cases of such complexity.

The actual day of receiving my cheque came around in March 2007. For 14 years I had built up to this, my anticipated light at the end of the tunnel. The office I had to attend to have the cheque signed off was in Sheffield, so I allowed Sam to have the day of off school to come with me. Everyone I knew was excited and relieved for me that this day had arrived. As they handed over the cheque to me, all £408,000 of it, all I wanted to do was to rip it up. In that office, it hit me like an exploding missile, that all I'd been through for the past 14 years of my life, every struggle, every painful moment, every section of my world falling apart, came down to this piece of paper. I bloody resented it and felt an extreme emptiness, it meant nothing in comparison. It was not the shiny rainbow and stars moment that I had held onto in my agonising wait. Where was that? If I'd have got it after 5 years, I wouldn't be here, I'd be dead. Compensation is not always the thing to get you through, it's about getting yourself through, people's perception is that compensation compensates, but it doesn't. Getting yourself into the right frame of mind is most important thing to do.

As I drove away from that office with Sam, I had visualised feeling elated and an inner sense that everything was now going to be okay and complete, that feeling was nowhere in my body or mind. In fact, it was the opposite and the thought of it repelled me. A strong desire to spend the money enveloped me on that drive home. An all or nothing, black or white approach of, "I'm going to blow it," sunk in, and so the empty, meaningless spending began.

It gave me a great excuse for a heavy drinking session at *The Rose*, to supposedly celebrate with my mates, if only they knew how I felt inside. One of the first major spends was on a 5 star holiday in Majorca with Pete and the kids. I genuinely wanted to thank him for all of the times he let us stay at his place in Tenerife. It had undoubtedly been a great support for me and the kids. Once home from the sunshine holiday and back to the real world, I started to spend on all kinds of stuff that I really didn't need. Another obsession was born. I did listen to reason and sought some financial advice and decided to put my money into a trust fund. This entitled me to still be able to claim for benefits. The fund states that this wealth is not designed for living expenses but as security for the remainder of your life. You are made a trustee of your own trust and in order to withdraw any of it you have to formally put in an application. Whilst that was a sensible decision, the flip side of this, is that I felt terrible through having the money and still claiming for benefits. It felt fraudulent and I experienced a lot of guilt.

In an attempt to view it as an investment for my future it seemed a good idea to research money making investments to grow my money. I followed the stocks and shares in a geek like style to educate myself and after a month I had made a profit of £5000 and calculations informed me that I could turn this into £60,000 annually so I reinvested. I took a large chunk of it, £275,000 to invest in stocks and shares. I became somewhat mildly obsessed with this also.

By July of 2007, I was craving my next adrenaline fix. A skydive fitted the bill! My parents were not impressed and I think others queried my sanity. Pete and I decided to do it together and found a company that did it from the ultimate height of 15,000 feet. We were set to do a tandem dive. I was hell bent on jumping out of a plane. I'd lost a lot of weight since my compensation as had started to look after myself more and was psyched up for this. There was one main requirement and that was the weather. We had been instructed that if it was a still day we wouldn't be allowed to take part. With having a disability we had to fly into the wind to allow us to fall and be caught, we could not land in the regular way. If there was no wind, the fall would be too fast. This particular day was still, I was gutted, but the weather can change so wait around all day watching the others make their dives from the sky. I watched with eager anticipation but also a sinking feeling of disappointment thinking I wouldn't be able to have my moment. Fortunately for me, the weather picked up by the end of the day – good old British weather. I was going to be on the very last plane of the day. I'd already been weighed in at 13 stone, it was the 13th of July and incidentally this specific plane was a number 13. The guy kitting me out with my parachute gear laughed and asked if I was superstitious. Superstitious or not, I was doing this! I was equally petrified and excited. On the edge of the small aeroplane, now attached to my skydive partner, I looked down and thought to myself what on earth was I doing?! Seconds later, we launched out of the plane's body and began to fall. It was incredible to fall so freely through the sky, the speed, the coldness, seeing the ground getting clearer in detail all added to the exhilaration. I now knew what it felt like to float, to feel weightless, it was amazing. Our bodies sprawled out and the force of the wind contorting our faces. We freefell the first 10,000 feet then my partner tugged and pulled open our chute. The last 5,000 feet was slower and more graceful, the ground getting closer and we landed safely into people's arms. I wanted to cry in sheer delight. That moment I realised that if I wanted to do things then I could, I was not bound by my wheelchair. Whilst up there, I felt no different to anyone else.

The following year, the stocks and shares skydived themselves. My life taking a further roller-coaster journey, too many downs though and not enough ups for my liking. The financial crash hit me hard and my original £275,000 investment decreased to £140,000. Painful. I felt very pressured. What had I done now? I'd not told a soul about still claiming benefits as I felt ashamed, but had no alternative now. With no other option, I stayed in my council flat. I had some cash behind me, enough to fund holidays and a few other luxuries. The next few months was a cycle of water skiing, going on holidays in the summer and for 2 months at Christmas. I'd go out on my own, then Sam and Abbi would come out. We stayed in an apartment in a safe resort. I'd do my usual, getting drunk, then in an evening Sam would push me back to go to bed before he'd go back off out.

Both myself and others thought that the compensation would be my, "bounce," but it turned out to be detrimental. I was so unhappy, it made me feel ten times worse as my perception and other people's had changed. I had this spare money but everyone was at work, so my answer was to go out and spend it. I'd buy jeans, tops, trainers, all pointless and buying for the sake of buying. It was almost as though I felt compelled to fritter the money away. I was filling in time, time that felt empty and aimless, there was still this black hole gnawing away at me, the void never being filled no matter what was poured into it. Drink, drugs, spending, hook ups, adrenaline activities, none of it meant anything and was only ever a very temporary release.

19
Dan Terry

It was in the run up to Christmas that year and I was in my regular drinking haunt, *The Rose*. A band was playing, adding to the merry atmosphere. One of the locals, Maggie, was a biker and she made a beeline for me across the bar. "I want to talk to you Jase, I need to give you something," and with that she thrust a business card into my free hand, the other one occupied by my pint glass. I glanced down and the name, "Dan Terry," and a phone number grabbed my attention. Smart looking card but it had no meaning to me. Maggie went on to explain how it had been passed onto her today with me in mind, through mutual connections. There had been a safety presentation that day delivered by this guy, Dan, who was a health and safety consultant. Part of the presentation was a talk from a guy called Ian that also used a wheelchair. Ian had been taken ill and could not attend and by chance, a neighbour of mine, Pete, worked at this place of the talk. Pete had thought of me and suggested that I was contacted as I may be interested. Apparently you could potentially earn a few hundred a day so it piqued my interest, after my recent financial woes. I tucked the card into my jacket pocket and carried on with the evening's drinking.

Nursing my hangover the following morning, I emptied my pockets from the night before in an effort to figure out how much I'd spent this time. Lots of loose change, fluff and then out tumbled the shiny business card. Staring hard at the card, I decide that I had nothing to lose and made a mental note to give him a phone call.

I met Dan in Newark, in a pub that I knew. He was a friendly chap and enquired about my story and was most interested in what had happened to me after my accident and the impact on my friends and family. He was very open and went into detail about how part of his job role entailed delivering presentations on behavioural safety. A powerful addition to this was for him to have a speaker that had actually experienced an accident. He asked me there and then if I was interested. It took me by surprise a little and I didn't feel confident in that I had a story to tell. I felt hesitant, but I heard myself agreeing to give it a go.

It wasn't long before Dan got me out on a job in the middle of nowhere in Lincolnshire. It was an onshore oil platform drilling rig, and so the room was full of roughnecks. I sat observing at the back of the room, the whole time thinking that this was definitely not for me as I watched Dan deliver an amazingly slick presentation bursting with confidence. How could I compete with that? What did I know?

A couple of weeks later Dan rang me up and invited me to another presentation he was giving. Something in me wanted to go, even though I could not envisage me ever up on the stage. I was the guy who had to drink several pints before I displayed any real confidence in a crowd. Unknowingly to me, beforehand, he introduced me at the end and brought me up to speak for about five minutes. He put me right on the spot leaving me with no real choice other than to do it, or I'd have looked a complete fool. My heart pounded the whole time and the five minutes seemed more like five hours in that kind of limelight. It sure was nerve racking.

Before Christmas arrived, I'd jetted off to Tenerife with the kids. I hated spending Christmas at home, as it was a reminder of what I didn't have and just depressed me. The sunshine always helped to with my darker moods and of course the socialising, involving much alcohol, was the big draw. It was a welcome escape at the end of the day and two months at a time was even better. One afternoon my phone rang, at the other end of the line was a voice I recognised, it was Dan. He was asking for my feedback on my speaking episode a week or so before. I told him that I hated it, was on holiday and that it was not my thing. I thought that would be the end of it. Christmas came and went and we entered into the New Year.

We'd only been home for a few days, getting acclimatised to the British winter, when Dan got in touch again. He clearly was not going to give up. He advised me to seriously consider his offer as my story could really help other people. It did make me think long and hard. Part of me had an inkling of desire but I was unsure and lacked the confidence and belief in myself. I went out with him again to another company and this time I spoke for longer in a fifteen minute slot. Again, it was very nerve racking. What was I thinking? At the end of the presentation, one of the men in the audience said that my talk had been the most powerful part of the whole presentation and thanked me for sharing my story. This boosted my confidence so much, it was just what I needed to hear to entice me to start working officially with

Dan. Each time, I would be bricking it, but he was paying me and something drove me forwards with it. I'd usually talk for between half an hour to an hour, then listen to Dan the rest of the time. Some of his talks felt beyond me, but I learned a lot and took a lot from them. I realised that the more I understood what he was saying, that it was echoing why I did what I had done. I knew that if I could marry that information with my personal story, I would create a greater impact myself. I started to hone my skills and my own presentation and actually began to enjoy it and also the new found confidence it gave to me. Over time, I got to know Dan quite well and his astute character. I secretly thought that he had planted that guy in the audience that time, to give me the push that he knew I needed.

Back out in Tenerife, I'd made some friends and one of them was with Kirsty, a young bar PR girl, obviously from my frequent drinking sessions. Most people would ask me when they first met me, what had happened to me? And to share with them the story of my accident. It was so refreshing for me because we never entered into this conversation. She didn't appear to notice and was not interested in what had already happened. She never even asked me how I was feeling but wanted to know what I'd been up to. She would say that all we have is now and that you cannot worry about the future either. She became a really good friend and I was inspired by her thinking. It was the first time that I started to think that I needed to put my energy and focus on the things that I could do instead of not do. This over a period of time, had a much needed influence on me.

At the beginning of 2011, I completed the HUET training required for me to be able to go offshore by helicopter to deliver my presentation to workers on an oilrig in the Irish sea. The idea had been discussed with Dave Clinton, a senior safety advisor as we sat having a meal and a few drinks as I was stopping in a hotel in Barrow delivering some presentations for the *Rampside Gas* terminal operated by *Centrica*. "Here's an idea," he said, "we should get you offshore to deliver your presentations on an oilrig, what do you think?"

Maybe fuelled by bravado from having a few drinks in me I readily took him up on the offer. We both knew it would take a lot of planning and a huge commitment by Dave to push his idea to reality, thankfully his bosses where keen on the idea and Dave started the rigorous amount of planning and organising a path through all the red tape to make it happen but he was determined and after a year since that meal on July 1st, I made the first of two trips in a helicopter to an oilrig. The trip was as secret as possible with only the ground crew who had been trained to get me off the helicopter and down into the mess area of the rig to deliver my presentation, the face on the workers as I wheeled in the room was classic, "how the hell have you got on an oilrig?" They asked. Dave then explained all the planning that had gone into making the trip possible, no shortcuts and I'd completed the Helicopter Underwater Evacuation Training, even asking for an extra dunk in the tank.

20
Outward and Inward Success

For someone to look at my life now, especially when compared to where it was just a few short years ago, they could not help but to see success. My business had gained momentum to the point where I had branched out on my own. In the first year I turned over £8000, the second year £40,000, and it doubled again by year three. My order book was getting busier month by month. I was drinking considerably less, I had my compensation and structured my time a lot more efficiently. My social life was active with many wonderful friends and my lovely kids were with me. So I was bewildered that the question I found myself asking time and time again was, "what was the meaning of it all?" Nothing felt as though it had any meaning and it was as though this speaking had become just another crutch.

People bought into my story as it's such an honest account and from the heart. For any speaking gig, I turn up in my jeans, trainers and hoody, I am who I am, an ordinary guy. I was working in Appledore in Devon when I first met Andy Forbes, we spoke in the yard at the company I was working at that day. He said that was what he liked about me and knew he would from just seeing me that day, he resonated with me, as out of his working suit he would be found donning similar casual clothing. After that job, which was well received, we became firm friends. He helped me to build my confidence further by reiterating to me how my speech needed to be told. I admired Andy as he was very knowledgeable and was of a senior position, so his words reassured me a great deal. I always struggled to see it in myself. One of my first big jobs in 2010 was at *Babcocks*, a huge organisation, and Andy's words gave me the belief that I could do it. Another big job was for IOSH. Whilst speaking there, a film company called *Outtakes* spotted me and the power behind my presentation. I joined forces with them to create my first film, A Fall from Height, a DVD that companies could use in their health and safety training. It really helped to amplify the marketing of my business, getting my face known and more bookings taken.

After some months of sub-contracting with Dan, and a twist of fate, he was offered an excellent job opportunity in a high-level position at consulting firm *Alexander Proudfoot*. He knew he had to accept and apologised for not being able to continue working with me. It was a shame and the old feelings of self-doubt crept back in but I had started to work with another consultant Matt Terry. So I went under Matt's wing instead providing a similar service. By now, my confidence had increased from the many talks I had given and the positive feedback received. It spurred me on. It was something that I was happy to continue and could feel myself getting used to it and believing in myself again.

By chance, Matt and I were meant to be working in Aberdeen. I'd got us a job at, *Sir Robert McAlpine*, through my website, it was a big client and we were going to be speaking in a theatre to 300 people. We planned to travel there on the train and meet up further along on the journey. Then on the day of the job, I received a call from Matt explaining that he'd hurt his ankle in a motorbike accident and could not make it. I had to think on my feet (not literally), and during the seven hour train trip to Scotland, I put together a presentation. I took the knowledge that I had from Dan and Matt's work, it wasn't as in depth, but covered some of the topics. I presented it twice that day, to 600 people and the feedback was great. It's funny how things turn out sometimes, it's just as though it was meant to be. As though a small event that could be seen as a negative, actually turns out to be the positive push that was needed. Just like when Dan had put me on the spot in the first instance.

Then there was another, as Matt took a new job out in the Middle East which really threw me in at the deep end. I am a quick learner, but my angle has always been, "I'm not a trained safety person." This has really helped my career as I'm different in that I'm not going in and telling the audience what they should be doing. I let them know what I did, which people relate to and they in turn think, if it could happen to Jason, it could happen to me. I've always been very self-critical of my presentation since day one and constantly improved it and it has evolved over time. I decided early on that if I was going to do this I had to talk about everything no matter how embarrassing for me. Initially this helped my nerves as talking graphically about wearing a leg bag, how you go to the toilet or the question nobody wants to ask, "does it still work," actually gave me a bit of confidence as I could see the audience squirm and feel uncomfortable. This sometimes could cause people to faint and this actually currently stands at 31, so I adjusted my story especially as my confidence grew as this was not the intended reaction. The, 'sex story,' as I call it always got a big laugh and while initially my presentations were mainly on sites in front of predominantly male audiences, I always embellished the story slightly to add to impact but there was an underlying reason, as I told of the impact this can have on relationships and the ability to have children. I had a contract with *Babcock Rail* and had visited many of their operational sites, but I was asked to do two days of presentations at the main offices in Hamilton. The audiences would be to a high percentage of female office staff, not sure of whether to add the usual content I decided on the first one to include the, 'sex story.' I was quite embarrassed but I got through it without too much giggling from the audience but I decided I would omit it from the next presentation to spare my embarrassment, and as I have always said, the audience you're sat in front of don't know if you cut something out, and indeed the second presentation in the afternoon went smoothly, or so I thought. Afterwards, while I was packing my things away, a female office lady came into the room and said she was a little disappointed with my presentation, this was still relatively early in my speaking career and I welcomed any kind of feedback that might help me progress, however I was not expecting what she said, "where was the sex story? My friend from this morning session said it was hilarious." She actually came into the next day's presentation to listen to it. The best part of this was she had taken my story home and sat and told her husband and made him look at his own relationship with safety.

It was a journey of exploration, this speaking career. As I began to see how I could potentially change one person's thinking or actions. How many others was that affecting or helping? By 2011, I knew it was something more. I didn't want the spotlight to be on me all of the time, as it was also about what had happened to my family and friends. With the change in ethos came a rebranding and the business became Proud2BeSafe Ltd, the meaning behind it was that you did your work but were proud to go home safely to your family. Soon enough, the order book was full and I was working 4 to 5 days a week. I had a new car on the drive and always had money in the bank but it didn't mean anything to me.

I was delighted to be asked to present at Stoke City Football Ground at a *Working Well Together* event, *WWT* was set up as a joint industry/HSE initiative. After finishing my presentation, I got to talk to some of the attendees who may ask further questions or share personal stories. However, on this occasion I met Dylan Skelhorn, he had driven all the way from Alloa, Scotland, for the event with the sole purpose of watching me speak plus to have a chat with me. He explained that he had been in a serious workplace accident just a few years before where he had fallen over 30 feet from a roof, sustaining, as he initially said, "nowhere near as bad as you, as I can still walk," but I listened to him talk about his life changing injuries leaving him 40% disabled. Although I still tease him, it must be at least 65%, and he needs to take a cocktail of drugs daily just for the pain, so he can at least function. Dylan's accident, like most was totally preventable and I encouraged him that his story needed telling, he then attended talks whenever I was in Scotland and then took the decision to start speaking. His presentation is highly regarded within the safety world and he now travels the UK sharing his story.

Dan had seen an article in a local paper of a builder who had suffered a fall from height leaving him paralysed from the waist down like myself but had no details apart from the article was in the *Gainsborough Standard*, a local newspaper in the Lincolnshire town. I set on a detective journey to find a contact number, in the end I found an address and sent a letter but unfortunately, he had sold the house and moved but the new occupier knew where he had gone, and so Paul Blanchard made contact. I travelled across to Gainsborough with Dan and we met Paul and his lovely wife Jenny, and they explained the circumstances to Paul's accident and the impact it had on them and his family and friends. It may sound callous, but I always listen for the angle or hook you might call it to a story, I had learned in my short time delivering presentations that it's not so much the story of the accident itself but more of the implications afterwards. Paul was an experienced builder running his own business but like many stories there was a chain of events that led to yet another avoidable accident. Paul, like Dylan now travels sharing his story of an older, experienced worker who after ignoring his own H&S concerns has paid the price and will spend the rest of his life using a wheelchair.

I take some fulfilment and pride seeing Dylan and Paul speak and I hope my guidance and advice has helped them and I'm always happy to help and offer advice and both have delivered presentations on behalf of *Proud2bSafe*.

It became too much for me to manage single handed, so in 2013, Abbi came to work for me full time. She had been helping me with my accounts since 2011, with her banking experience it really helped relieve the workload. Now she took over the administration side altogether which was desperately needed. I worked hard and always took August and January off, January would be a trip to Tenerife but I didn't use the time to relax, I continued the partying lifestyle that used to dominate my week. It was during this phase that I decided to leave my council flat where I had lived for about twenty years, those four walls had many stories to tell. I moved into a bungalow, my first ever private home and was able to pay for it outright. One of my oldest friends, Jo, rented it from me after I moved out, along with her partner and baby, Beau. It was a great way to help a friend, we went back a long way. One day she came round to my new house with something to tell me. I knew from her face it was serious and it crumpled as she dissolved into a flood of tears, in-between sobs she muttered the word, "cancer." I was mortified too, and joined her crying bout. Flashbacks of our fun times entered my mind but she reassured me that she was going to be okay as they had caught it in the early stages. She was determined to fight it. Wayne, her partner had told us that she was sicker than we thought, which was hard to hear when we were down at the pub and seeing Jo's upbeat and positive mentality.

My work was fulfilling me more, for the first time in a very long time, I felt a sense of self-worth. I began to take more pride in what I was doing and enjoyed the sense of achievement and of making a worthwhile difference to people's lives. I hadn't felt this feeling since back in my twenties when I had my dream job as a sign writer. My personal life still borrowed itself to some chaos, with drunken affairs and without any sign of me being ready to be in a relationship, this was my stumbling block. In all honesty, I was terrified, I'd achieved so much but the belief was that if I were to get my heart involved with another person and it didn't work out then I'd fall off of a cliff. I just could not let that happen and I made the decision of a firm no, why strive for more when you're okay with what you've got? As much as people commented on all that was missing was a partner I had this overwhelming fear. My drinking had calmed right down to once a week, not feeling the need as much for the release of my pent up tensions.

Out of the blue in October 2014 a letter arrived on my doormat, a rather official looking letter. Irvine, Abbi's fiancēs brother had recently completed jury duty and I convinced it was that. I was too busy to take time out now I thought as I tore the envelope open. I stopped in my tracks when I read just the first paragraph... I'd been nominated for an MBE. Oh my God! How amazing, but why me, after such a short space of time? Moments later, the penny dropped... wait a minute, it wasn't a nomination it was an actual award, I'd got it! When the compelling words had sunk in a little more, I read that the award was for Services to the Construction Industry - Health and Safety, and I was sworn to secrecy. I took the letter and exciting news over to my parents to share with them, they were over the moon. I told them it was just a nomination and not to say anything just in case they started telling people as I had been sworn to secrecy, a week before Christmas, the local newspaper called me, they wanted to interview me for the newspaper. They get told of award winners by the press agency, but I'd left the letter at my mum's house and needed to retrieve it for when the reporter came around to see me. So there I was, inventing a fabricated tale to my parents to snatch my letter back without them realising and keeping my lips sealed - not an easy task, believe me! I confided in Abbi and Sam and they were thrilled, to see their beaming smiles meant everything. I was photographed and interviewed ready for the story to run when the announcements were made on New Year's Eve.

Dan had also taught me about the Law of Attraction, and I really began to see the power of it showing up in my life. More and more, I would focus on the things that I wanted in my life and learned to filter out the not so good stuff. It was challenging at first but the results were astounding, and when I reflected back, I saw a long pattern of this in my life. Where the focus goes, energy flows¬ - an adage that spoke massive amounts of truth to me. Kirsty had mentioned this in our conversations too and I could see why she never focussed on the past and why her general attitude was different to many others. At Dan's suggestion, I should start small, he asked, "what really irritates you?"

I replied, "traffic lights always seemingly to be on red when I approached."

He laughed and then told me, "you should visualise the traffic light being on green, really visualise just sailing through," and it just started to happen, every time I got to the lights they would be on green. Wow was it really that simple to have control over things purely through thought? Well in reality, I had quite simply just started to pay more attention to the 50% times the light would be on green and not the 50% they would be on red. More and more, I started to focus on the things that I wanted in my life and simply learned to filter out the not so good stuff.

Brilliant! I truly began to shift my beliefs and one of my new formed beliefs was that anything can happen and anyone can achieve anything they want to, including me. When something good occurred it would cheer me up and keep me lifted for days on end, it had deep meaning because the thing that I had desired had come true. This would wow me, and the thought that led on would be – what else can I achieve? In the past, I'd have fought like crazy to get myself back to feeling neutral, a lot of effort was required, now I searched for the good in a bad situation, as there always is some and when you pinpoint that, focus your energy on it you attract more into your reality. It could happen today, tomorrow or months later, but sure as anything, it appeared. When I had been frittering away my compensation and purchasing stuff instantly, it had been meaningless. This was the spark that changed so much for me, as it had a ripple effect as I passed this onto others in my world, as they could to me. It felt like the ingredients that magic is made of, seriously.

I have made many new friends through my business and travelling all over the UK and as we have become close friends we now also socialise outside of work. Jim Smith who works for *Scottish Water* became my chaperone as I travelled all over Scotland delivering my presentation across the whole business in 2013/14. He has also become good friends with my kids and circle of friends and pays regular visits and he calls me his only English friend in his top friends list, which is a great accolade from a proud Scotsman.

Andy Forbes who worked for *Babcock*'s and was my initial contact with the company in 2010, has also become a great friend, if I'm in Scotland we often meet up for a meal with his wife Jackie. Andy has a cracking sense of humour and is a great friend, but he is always there with support and advice if needed. Although asking his advice on what to wear at a *Babcock* function wasn't my wisest idea, I rang him to ask what, 'smart casual,' meant on the invite: suit or shirt and tie? I had thought that was the end of the matter, but Andy decided to tell the room of over 100 people later that evening at the function taking great enjoyment out of my embarrassment.

I also have worked for several years for *Babcock* at the Royal Navy base in Devonport, Plymouth and again making some great friends down there and usually at the end of a week's presentations on a Thursday we would head out for a meal with the SCIT team, John, Mike, Steve, Naomi and a few others would always have a good meal, a few beers and a good laugh. One night, we had had a few too many and they decided to take me to a famous local landmark *Capt. Jaspers*, a food vendor on the Barbican, for a Jasperizer, which is not a random cocktail, but actually a local tradition ¬- a burger - drunkenly we set off with Mike offering to push me in my wheelchair. A mixture of being a bit tipsy and a cobbled path, I fell out my wheelchair, they were all mortified but I was picked up quickly and we continued on to get our burger, although we still tease Mike about how he was responsible for tipping such an important person out his chair.

21
My Princess and a Castle

During 2014, Abbi announced that she was getting married. Fergus, her fiancé is of Scottish heritage on his mum Christine's side and they opted for a small wedding in Scotland. When Abbi was a little girl she had nothing much materialistically from me but she had, in fact, everything. My time and my love. She was always my princess and from being the young girl with pigtails she always said that when she grew up she wanted to get married in a castle. A true little girl's dream fairy tale. It saddened me at that time to think that there was no way that would ever happen, I was from a council estate and not even working anymore since my accident. Knowing what I did now, we put the intention out there into the universe and let whatever was going to happen, happen.

Since the days of my accident and marriage split, the two families had become a, "them," and, "us," scenario. That period of time had torn us apart and Sam and Abbi grew up with two separate lives with each parent. This was a concern for Abbi when she was making her wedding plans and was conscious that these bad memories would crop up on the day when the two families were finally reunited together under one roof.

My business had done especially well that year and I was overjoyed to tell Abbi that the princess could have her happy ever after castle. The joy on her face was worth everything and it felt so incredible to think that this was going to happen for her. It was only a matter of time before the perfect setting was discovered, Dundas Castle in Edinburgh. We instantly fell in love with the pale bricked towers set in the beautiful grounds as a few of us went to visit. Steeped in incredible history it was all we had dreamed of and more. Lord Jack, the proprietor, made us very welcome and as we viewed the part of the castle we would be staying at he instructed us to treat it as our own whilst we were there.

I anticipated an amazing special day but also shared a fleeting concern about if the two families were to clash. Abbi, Fergus and I travelled up a couple of days before, to settle in and ensure that the arrangements ran smoothly. A lot of the family joined us the day before the wedding itself, and the buzz of growing excitement could be felt from everyone as we enjoyed our lavish surroundings. I had so wanted this for my daughter and all we had been through as a family. I could still see traces from Abbi's expressions, wondering if it was all going to go smoothly, and then a car arrived with Paula, her family and Sam, followed swiftly by my parents and sister. As we all stood in the grand foyer, it felt peaceful. It was as though as invisible line had been drawn in the sand, we could be friends again and peace had been made. What had happened all those years ago would never be forgotten but it was time to release any resentments.

The day itself, March 25th, was simply the best day ever. I'd always feared this day for the part where I would not be able to walk my daughter down the aisle. As I watched her walk gracefully down the huge cascading staircase, followed by the bridesmaids, she looked so beautiful. I felt tears pricking my eyes as I listened to the Ellie Goulding melody in the background as I waited in my chair at the bottom. Up until that moment, I had imagined it was going to be difficult, but as she held my hand, it was far from awkward. As we listened to the Ellie Goulding's, *How Long Will I Love You*, in the background. We made our way into the stunningly decorated wedding room where all of our guests were waiting patiently. My heart and face matched my princess's smile. This feeds back into the thought process of focussing on what you can do instead of cannot do. My daughter got married in the castle of her childhood dreams, it never would have happened if I'd not have had my accident. Now there's a thought.

The Rose and Crown hosted a wonderful party and disco for my friend Jo in April of 2015. She had been through two very rough years of cancer treatment and breast surgery. She was a tough cookie and loved life. Not once in those two years had she moaned. She was the life and soul and was in her element that night, hugging and planting kisses on everybody in the room, bursting with happiness.

The previous December 31st, my MBE award had been made public and it was six months later in the June that I actually went for the ceremony at Buckingham Palace. My dad and Abbi accompanied me, the three of us dressed up to suit this once in a lifetime occasion. It was a magnificent palace inside, none of us were sure what to expect, only what your imagination conjures up from snapshots seen on the television. Such decadence and it instantly made you feel important. On arrival, I was ushered into a side room whilst dad and Abbi congregated with other guests in a hall. I was excited yet nervous as we were given instructions on what to do etiquette wise as my memory really is not the best. I was one of about 150 other awardees and the only one who said that they didn't understand the set of commands, so it was repeated again. Gulping, I was still struggling to take it in but I told myself that I'd watch and repeat what those in front of me in the queue did. I don't think I nodded exactly when I was supposed to, but Prince Charles knew all about me, I was quite taken aback and humbled by the whole experience. His Royal Highness questioned me about my work and particularly about the aircraft carrier when I was a safety ambassador for the entire project. I did presentations to the workforce especially during the construction phase when working at height was a huge concern. I also got the chance to go on board during construction which was a huge honour to say I've actually been on board. He shook my hand and handed me my award and then photographs were captured for the newspapers. I was in awe really and wondered why I was so deserving of something so prestigious after just doing what I had for seven years, I was just a normal bloke. I whisked Abbi and my dad off to *The Savoy* where we toasted with very expensive bottles of champagne, no expense spared that day! Back home, my award took pride of place in my lounge and every time I pass by it, I smile to myself.

In the May 2014, Sam also came to work for me, initially setting up my IT and general help, I persuaded him to talk for a few minutes as I knew it would be a powerful angle to my presentations. He reluctantly agreed but he spoke not about our relationship as he knew it would be too emotional, however he spoke about his grandad, my ex-father in law Keith, on how my accident was still affecting his life, and the guilt he still feels with the fact he was my boss at the time. In safety there is a saying, "the ripple effect," it's about how wide the impact goes after an accident. Keith still has nightmares about watching me fall, a quarter of a century later. Sam, although enjoying the closeness of being with his dad all week working away from home, found listening to and reliving the impact daily became too much for him, and he resigned a year later in May 2015. Sam later re-joined later that year running the social media side of the business for a couple of years.

As Sam left the company an old friend joined, Sean Toon, my old neighbour from my childhood, the one who left his flat after my release from hospital, joined *Proud2bSafe*, initially as my driver/assistant. My workload currently was taking its toll on my health as I was presenting 4-5 days a week and with all the travelling on top I was verging on exhaustion. As soon as Sean started working for me and listening to my presentations daily on the long road trips, he started to share stories of my accident but from his and my friends' perspectives, how difficult it had been for them and how helpless they felt watching my life implode. Knowing how valuable Sam's input on my presentations had been I encouraged Sean to speak but he was very reluctant, but after a lot of persuasion he agreed to give it a try. Initially he refused to stand and with his head bowed he spoke for about two minutes, but like Dan had known when he first heard my story, I knew it would have an impact. Today Sean stands and speaks with confidence several times during my presentation and is always spoken to afterwards by people who hadn't realise the implications accidents have on the friends of the injured person. In 2018 Sean was awarded a Guardian Angel Award, from *RoSPA* for his services to safety.

While working for a client in East Anglia, I was asked to meet a chap called Matt Hazelton, his groundworks company had been involved in a tragic accident resulting in the deaths of four people. The victims were all closely known to Matt, as two were his younger brothers and two of his best friends. The man we met that day was broken, with the help of his friend they told of the story of the accident and the devastation this had caused and the victims all came from the same small area not far from Bury St Edmunds. I am humbled to have been a part of Matt's journey. I find it incredible he is able to share such a harrowing story, his talk, 'Four Friends,' is a story that leaves no stone unturned, at the end Matt walks off stage to the music that was played at the funeral, to stunned silence in the audience as everyone needs the time to compute all they have heard in the 45 minute presentation. The transformation in Matt himself, but also those people close to him has made the enormous effort worthwhile, and he has become a huge part of, not just *Proud2bsafe*, he has become a great friend. We were overjoyed when Matt won the SHP 'Rising Star Biggest Impact Award' in 2017 for his unselfish contribution to safety.

On a very sad note, it was around this time that I discovered that my friend Jo was slipping away. Unbeknown to us all, the cancer had always been a lot more aggressive than Jo had ever revealed. I think the party, just two months prior, had been her way of saying goodbye to everyone. Her cancer had accelerated and turned into the worst type that there was no coming back from. She had periodically gone into hospital but due to her buoyant outlook none of us had guessed. I was working in Manchester in the July and Wayne called me to say that I needed to come and see Jo in hospital. I felt bad as I was working away but said I could go that evening to Nottingham to visit her, then drive back to Manchester for the second day of presenting to my client. After giving the logistics more thought, I decided the better option would be to stay put that night and as soon as I'd finished working the next day, I'd go directly to the hospital. It was shocking when I got to the hospital's private room, as it was no longer the Jo I knew and loved. She was hooked up to morphine, heavily bloated and was in and out of consciousness. I spoke to her dad and he explained how she was now mostly out of it. I wheeled my chair next to her bedside and reached for her hand, squeezing it as a tear fell onto my cheek. She roused and asked me where the hell I'd been the day before, she had known (typical Jo). I silently said my goodbye and felt my insides crushing with deep sorrow. Her dad said to me as I left that it would just be family now, as all of her close friends had been to see her and she was not going to hold on much longer.

The following week, I was just about to go on stage at a company in Heathrow when my phone rang and Charlotte's name flashed up, Jo's best friend. I just knew before I answered the call. We had lost Jo. I felt a sense of deep sadness but it was also a strange sense of relief for her that she'd passed. She had battled it every day, bless her, and never made anyone else suffer. She now had found peace after being strong for everyone else.

July came and we all gathered for Jo's funeral. It all came out just how seriously ill she had been from her diagnosis. She had clearly been such a positive and tenacious lady that she had added on years to her prognosis. Her spirit had known that she could not beat the cancer but she did her damnedest to make it as happy, fulfilled and as long as possible. She fought as long as she could to be with her loved ones, Wayne and Beau, and died at a very young 38 years. The only bad months we saw were at the end when she became so ill she could not hide it anymore. To me, that's true resilience, the epitome of what resilience is. She was an inspiration to us all. Each year we have a celebration during July for her at *The Rose*, to celebrate her legacy.

That same month, through a chance conversation with Kirsty, she asked me if she could try out some new coaching techniques with me. I had come to the decision that I did want to find a way to meet someone to share my life with. I was ready but did not know how, with this defence that I had constructed to preserve myself. We decided to make a weekend away out of it after I admitted that I didn't think I'd be able to open up properly until I'd had a couple of drinks. I found myself in Scotland again after enjoying the stunning scenery so much for Abbi's wedding. Kirsty and I dined out in the evening, shared a few drinks and a very honest conversation followed. I opened my heart and said how much I really would like to meet someone but how fearful I was to the point of stopping me. She asked me what was the worst that could happen? When I shared my answers, we discussed them through and it began to alleviate some of my worries. By the next morning, I had a whole new perspective on the situation. My greatest fear could actually be my greatest life and right now I was blocking it. From this, Kirsty suggested that I needed to start to look for somebody, put it out there, make myself open to the possibility. As like with anything, if you tell yourself that you're not going to meet anybody, you won't. It's that simple. I felt as though I'd lost the best part of twenty years as all I'd done was frantically finding ways to cope. In hindsight, it was a twenty year blur.

It never ceases to amaze me, but from that meeting in July and what I decided upon, by August the universe had delivered.

22
Having It All

That girl from the party all of those years ago, the girl I'd kissed, well completely out of the blue, a comment from her appeared on a social media channel, after being virtual friends for some time. We got chatting and met up for a coffee. We really hit it off and realised we had interests in common and there was still that magic spark. It was great fun too, as we relived the teenage years, and all of the highs and lows those years bring. A relationship developed quickly from that coffee, as there had always been something there and it was as though a missed opportunity from the past was now presenting itself and we both embraced it full on. Two months later and we were a solid item, and wanted to be together as much as possible. It was wonderful and I could not hardly believe that I now had all that I had wanted and asked for. I literally had to pinch myself, was I really the same guy from just a few years ago? The one who survived in a haze of alcohol and other substances? And the one who never dared to truly show his feelings and commit to another woman again?

My family and friends were really happy for me but I also sensed a brooding concern from them all. I knew what they were thinking - what would happen to me if it all went wrong? I didn't want to consider this, as I now focussed on the good and let the rest go as much as I could. Abbi and Sam were both initially delighted for me, to see their dad happy and finally with someone after years of trying to persuade me. At first everything was fantastic. My girlfriend and I had so much in common both having grown up children and I connected further as she came to work for me as a business development manager for a couple of days a week to really push the business forward. By 2016 she was on the team full time. Not all ran smoothly though, as feathers were ruffled in the office. Her and Abbi clashed, Abbi felt put out as she'd had great responsibility running the business whilst I'd been on the road and delivering our presentations. Then along came this new woman with her ideas and influence. I probably didn't do enough to diffuse the building tensions, I felt stuck as piggy in the middle of my daughter and girlfriend. I valued them both greatly.

A dream of mine was to live in a house in the middle of nowhere, it struck me as peaceful, maybe that was what I hankered for after the years of chaos I had lived through? My girlfriend and I wanted to live together, so we made the move to sell each of our houses and move in together. In a very short succession, I'd sold my bungalow within a week of being on the market and my mum actually found the perfect place in a brochure, had circled it and as soon as I caught sight of it, I knew it was the one I wanted to live in. As we went for the viewing and pulled up on the big driveway, it confirmed it was the place I had dreamed of, before I'd even gone through the front door. Everyone we knew were both delighted but thought that our plans were going far too fast, it had been a whirlwind since that first coffee. Whilst I am prone to impulsivity, I also felt as though I had a lot of making up to do, for all of that lost and unhappy time. Life was for living and living I was! I did understand where these folks were coming from though, they only had my best interests at heart and that was never a negative. What my partner didn't quite seem to grasp was that in her absence, my family and friends had been through 22 years of turmoil with me. As much as I relayed to her all that had happened to me and the impact it had had on everyone, she hadn't witnessed it or experienced it herself. When one of them would enquire to how it was going with us, she took a bit of offence, when really they just knew how bad it had been for me.

It was very exciting the day I received the call from the estate agents to say that our offer on the house had been accepted and we began to make our moving plans like a couple of over excited teenagers. As my bungalow had sold so quickly, I had to move out for a month prior to our house being available. Up until this stage, we had not had one argument. The days had been filled with laughter, catching up on old memories and creating new ones, it was fantastic. The only trouble was, my girlfriend's house hadn't yet sold, so for the first time in years, things became tight financially. We hung on though, tightened our belts and got through that tough period. On December 6th we had moved in, not that much over a year since we had been reunited.

I was very happy as we settled into our new place, I really did now have it all. It was a spacious home, perfect for me and we made plans to adapt parts of it over time, there was nothing major which was a bonus for me. It was just as I had imagined it in my wildest dreams and now I had a special partner to share it with too. When we first met, our conversation had led to the friendships we both had. I explained that I had a lot of female friends, nothing romantic in the equation, purely platonic but they had been there for me over the years. She said that it wasn't a problem, but over the coming months, it seemed obvious that it was. I spoke to Kirsty, who was one of my closest female friends at the time, a lot less, as I knew my girlfriend didn't like my involvement. One day in April, a photo of Kirsty, appeared on my Facebook timeline. It dated back to the year previously, before I'd got in touch with my partner, however she was convinced otherwise. After seeing this, she declared that she did not trust my friend but without much more of a reason. I remembered how challenging relationships could be, but I had not been in one for over twenty years so I just sort of shrugged it off and thought we had put it behind us. We got on with our lives and I was still very happy in the new home. During October, there was a big, dramatic kick off, again involving Kirsty so I decided to distance myself a lot more to keep the peace and to keep my partner happy. Kirsty was very understanding and said that she was still my friend, whatever was happening in my world. That was that.

Other cracks began to appear in our relationship after Christmas, it was not the best start to 2017. My partner had decided to set up her own business whilst going back to work for me part time. It had taken off some of the heated pressure between her and Abbi, but financially it not ideal as she was finding it hard to financially fund her venture to get it up and running. We converted the garage at home into an office for her to work from, but things didn't appear to be happening quickly enough and there was a huge issue with getting a broadband connection suitable enough to run a business of that type seeing as we lived so remotely. I found it hard to give her the support she needed but I was still working away most of the week.

Sam was still having some troubles, so after the coaching with Kirsty I arranged for him to have some sessions with a friend of mine, Matt Coleclough. With Sam, it mostly stemmed back to when he was about ten years old and he found out why I couldn't play football with him, what had happened to me when I fell off of the ladder. In his little mind he believed that he'd missed out compared to Abbi. While Abbi would be content with playing inside, baking, colouring in and quieter pastimes, Sam was a typical lad and wanted to be outside kicking a ball around and doing lots of physical activity. Of course I couldn't fulfil that dream for him, so he believed that he'd lost out on the things dads did with their sons. His behaviour became more challenging as he got older and maybe I didn't help matters as after I received my compensation, he was 15 and I tried to make up for it. I thought that Sam had missed out too and felt bad for him. I bought him a lot of stuff, holidays abroad, a motor bike, the latest mobile phone and all it had done was to make his behaviour worse. He always said that Abbi had not lost out on too much unlike him. I admit, I probably should have done things differently but I was still secretly struggling myself. After dropping out of college, I sent him up to Andy's for a year at the ski centre in Rochdale. He lived there, learnt to drive a speedboat and wakeboard and I had hoped that he would become more independent. Sadly, on his return there seemed there was no change in him, which meant that he drifted in and out of jobs aimlessly and was unemployed for a while. I continued to support him but it fractured our relationship a little. Then he was 19 and living with me, I sometimes had to work away overnight. On one occasion, I returned home to a trashed house after a party he'd held. Probably nothing more than we all did when we were younger but it really hurt me, it seemed he was very angry with me on quite a deep level. I had to ask him to leave as it just was not working between us. I paid for him to move into his own flat, but he still struggled. He found it hard to grasp life, to know what he wanted and to focus on. Sam admits now that he had lived in the past continuously and felt grieved by what had happened, and I was always attempting to steer him onto the right path from the wrong one.

Matt had a company called Mindsafe. He was a psychotherapist after having his own mental health issues as a younger person, Matt and his team provided a specialist service in the treatment of anxiety disorders. They had a unique approach which took a combination of psychology, mindfulness, neuroscience, biofeedback and wellbeing. It looks at issues such as anxiety and depression in a slightly different way. I thought I was taking Sam to see Matt but once we arrived, Sam asked me if I'd go into the session with him. I was a bit surprised but happy to support him. The session was incredible, Sam was a keen book reader especially on these self-help books and connected straight away with Matt's explanations but in the end, I think I actually got more out of it initially than Sam did. As we drove home, I was lit up with new realisations and answers from all of my own life. I was amazed and so grateful to have this new and exciting knowledge. As I mentioned how I'd used my virtual scale and kept myself at number 5 for years, Matt explained that I'd been avoiding situations and blocking unpleasant things out. I'd not been living, I'd been surviving and had not been prepared to take any chances in life. I hoped that Sam would start to see himself and his thoughts differently like I had especially with some more time with Matt. When I got home, my girlfriend was waiting up for me. As she heard me passionately recalling all what I'd heard in that session all she found to say was, "oh, that's another thing you've heard then that's going to change your life."

One cold Thursday March night, I'd got home from a long and busy day at work, out on the road, with much travelling to and from the speaking engagement. I collapsed on the sofa to relax next to my girlfriend when my phone rang. It was Kirsty. She'd been coaching Sam for a while and during this time we didn't speak at all. Sam had explained that she needed to keep her professional distance, which I could see was only fair. Understanding this, I ignored the call as I knew it would be connected with Sam. Thinking no more about it, I said I was going for a shower to freshen up before we had dinner. A few minutes later, when I came back into the lounge, instead of us sitting down to eat dinner, I was cross questioned about Kirsty. She had been into my phone, to figure out how often I was still in touch with Kirsty. There were no records as I'd deleted them all after the arguments we'd previously had about her. There was silence for most of the evening. I started to go over things in my head, I'd been trying to do the right thing by protecting them both, staying friends with Kirsty and keeping my partner happy. I had a clear conscience and didn't think it was a major issue. We had a bit of a row the next day but I was not about to apologise as I'd not done anything wrong. It obviously was for her though, as on the Monday morning I went out to work as usual, I would be away all week but before I had come home she had moved out. I could not believe it, there was no discussion, no nothing. My mind cast back to her remark just three weeks before after the session with Matt. Yes, she was right, it had changed my life. I'd begun to change my thinking and as quick as she had come into my life, now she was gone.

23
The Final Chapter

I was still upset when my girlfriend left, it was only natural to have those feelings. I was working away from home and there were text messages and calls back and forth between us but I kept thinking on what Matt had said and I rang him back up. It was a very helpful reminder to be told that I could choose to spend all of my time worrying but that I needed to focus on what to do now. I was away until Friday, then had a meeting with my friend and mentor Tim Marsh, to discuss some ideas I had for taking my business forward and when we met he asked me how my girlfriend was. I revealed that she had left me. When he asked if I was okay, I explained that I hadn't thought of it too much and that yes I thought that I was okay. I was relating my circumstances back to what Matt had taught me. As Tim was a psychologist, he gave me a quizzical look, asked me again and then he announced that, yes I was ok and coming from such a highly regarded psychologist, so I concluded that I must be. We continued with our business meeting - it had definitely been a strange week.

On the drive back from Manchester unhelpful thoughts plagued me a little. Sean, one of my close friends, had come to work for me as a driver as the nature of my work meant that a lot of time is spent travelling. He also did short talks from his perspective. I dropped Sean off at the village and then had another ten miles to go to reach my home. Driving down the dual carriageway, the window wipers clearing the windscreen from the torrential rain, I began to think, "what have I done? I've left my bungalow to move to this house in the middle of nowhere and am now saddled with a mortgage." It upset me, and I could feel myself drifting back to feelings of loss. Once I pulled onto my long tree lined drive and drove up to my property, the rain had died down. My headlights flashed onto the front of my building, illuminating the front door, with that I smiled to myself and said, "this is all yours now."

The following month, April 2017, was my 49th birthday, only weeks after the split. Abbi suggested me having a party but I didn't want to do it, I didn't feel in the mood. However she insisted, and I'm glad that she pushed the idea. I had a big gathering at my place, with friends and family helping me to celebrate, it turned out to be a great night, and one of the memories I was happy to keep.

My ex-girlfriend and I stayed in contact for about a year. She blamed me for everything, it was all my fault. Initially I'd receive angry texts and it would trigger me into responding and dragged me down. I kept in contact with Matt a fair bit, as his advice really made a difference for me. He challenged my thinking and asked what was I going to achieve by responding this way? I could never win the argument, she thought she'd been hurt by me and I was busy defending my position, it was a stalemate and only encouraging bad feelings. At his suggestion, I changed tactics, and began to agree with everything she said. I explained that I hadn't meant to hurt her. The texts did become friendlier and then I'd question myself if I'd been too stubborn again like when Abbi left at 15, should I try to reconcile, it had all ended so fast but whenever we texted, I'd then spend the next few hours or a day or so reflecting back on what I'd lost, reliving all of the anger and pain again on why she had left.

Basically, I was punishing myself. Matt asked me, what were the positives of my relationship? Well I'd been drinking too much and she'd said I should think about my health, so I cut down and felt a lot better for it. And it was my ex that brought me to be living in my dream house. So that was all I needed to concentrate on, make this my memory of this relationship. Then a close friend suggested that I just cut all ties with her. This seemed a bit harsh but I saw the reasoning behind it, why continue the contact if all it did was cause pain? So overnight I deleted all of her messages, cut her off on social media and blocked her phone number. It was such a hard decision, I'd wanted to remain friends, but I saw that no good was going to come from that, except more pain. If every time I spoke to her I'd feel sad, it would make me reflect on the past and the only way to move forwards was to let go. It made a huge difference to me and I was able to put it behind me and focus on the now again.

A few months later, I was out in Newark with Fergus's parents to see a band. It was a band that my ex and I used to like but that was it, I had no thoughts on whether she'd be there or not. I spotted one of her friends across the crowded pub, and then another. I came to the conclusion that she must be there and felt very conscious that she was stood somewhere near me in the crowd. I quickly reminded myself of Matt's words, what was the point of worrying about it, I was out with friends. I did see her after a while and as she came over, she asked, "you've blocked me, haven't you?"

It felt wrong to be like this, I should go talk to her, buy her a drink, ask if she is okay but what would it achieve? Just more questions, more time spent going over things, if only I had said this or not said that. So, with Matt's advice I completely forgot she was there and had a great night watching one of my favourite bands with my friends.

I now use this analogy: If someone is going onto a computer, they delete stuff and then it goes into a recycle bin and it stays there. Then sometimes, something happens in the future and they can go back into the recycle bin and install it back onto their computer. The best thing that you can do is to go into the recycle bin and delete it for good. So going forwards, whenever anyone mentioned my ex, instead of me getting angry and sad about it, I focus on where I live, my dream home and I am healthier for not drinking as much. I'm grateful for having had that relationship because of what it has brought me.

After Jo had died in 2015, Sarah, my cousin I was so close to and who I thought of as more than a cousin, was diagnosed with ovarian cancer. She had two young boys. She had a slightly different mindset to Jo initially, so I took the approach Jo had taken and told Sarah that we were not talking about the "c" word. All of the family were talking about it and dwelling on it. Sarah really appreciated it and loved spending time with me. We'd sit drinking coffee in my conservatory talking about anything and everything except cancer. It was an escape for her. Towards the end of her battle, she moved into a lovely hospice and was very calm. She slipped away during November. She was buried about four graves away from Jo, so I visit them both at the same time and always have a chat with them both.

Business began to thrive again as Abbi went back to running the show. From that conversation on that Friday with Tim, the week my ex left, I went into partnership with him, and *Anker & Marsh* was formed. The aim was to take it to a market leader in looking at health, safety and wellbeing and it soon began to go from strength to strength in the planning stage. I wouldn't have taken this step if I had stayed with my ex, as we were going on a different path.

I'd lost touch with Dan a bit over the years, we were both always so busy in our careers, but I remained a part of his social circle. I had a phone call around this time to say that his cancer was back. He said that he was doing it again, he was going to beat it. I didn't even stop to question that as I knew the infectious kind of positivity the guy oozed. Nineteen years ago, he'd been diagnosed with Non-Hodgkin Lymphoma and he had blatantly refused to die. He beat it with his powerful mind-set and filling his days with laughter. I texted him to see how his treatment was going a few weeks later, plus it was his birthday. He said that he couldn't speak right now as he was in Damon's, his favourite restaurant, having Ribs, his favourite meal. His family was so important to him.

I began to create a new presentation, with the focus on resilience with the work I had planned with Tim. Some powerful examples I used were how in 1974, Shirley who had a son critically ill with a condition similar to leukaemia - Wiskott-Aldrich syndrome, a rare inherited blood disorder - set up a system where a person could go and register to donate their bone marrow known as *The Anthony Nolan Trust*. There are now 700,000 people on that register. Her son didn't survive but imagine how many lives she has gone on to help save? When Stephen Lawrence was murdered in 1993, his mum, Doreen, was absolutely broken hearted. From that unimaginable trauma she knew that she had to do something, all through her grief she became determined that there had to be some good to come out of it. She set up the *Stephen Lawrence Charitable Trust* which supports young people and creates social change. It's about finding the chink in the armour and using that in an inspiring way to create positive transformation.

For years, when I thought about the day I became a grandad, I was terrified. I imagined that I'd have to relive all of the things that I couldn't do with my own kids and how upsetting that was. I really got myself worked up, but that was my thoughts about the future, the, "what if's." I had been delighted when Abbi announced that she was pregnant, but then became very anxious again. When, on Feb 3rd 2017, Elle came into this world, I had started to think a little differently. It was an amazing occasion and we all fell in love with this gorgeous little girl immediately. From very early on, Elle knew I was different. When she sat on my knee, she sat perfectly still, whereas with everyone else she wriggles around like a typical young child, into everything and curious with the world. My relationship with her is wonderful, I never thought it would be possible - it's purely mindset. Another part of my new talk is, "imagine you couldn't walk on the beach with your granddaughter..." Just a few weeks ago, the family all went to Sutton-On-Sea. The weather wasn't great but we hired a chalet on the beach to spend time with Elle. Fergus's dad, Paul, took Elle on the beach, just walking and playing and I was happy. Once upon a time I wouldn't have been, it would have broken me emotionally. I have an electric scooter attachment that fits onto my wheelchair so then after Elle's time with Paul, she sat on my knee, held tight and we whizzed up and down on the promenade having great fun. I now choose to focus on what I can do with her.

I turned 50 this year and decided to hold a big party for family and friends, Abbi had organised one of my favourite bands to play, it was fantastic to see some of my old friends especially off Oak Avenue, the street that holds such happy memories for me. We had a great night then back to mine, to Aces nightclub, yes I converted the offices into a room to party and we did into the early hours. I owned a sore head in the morning but I had had such a great night and spent the next day opening all of the wonderful cards and presents. August saw the *Ankerfest2* in the grounds of where I live, with band and disco, I get so much happiness watching my family and friends enjoying themselves although those who camped out in their tents on probably the first wet night in months may disagree, but tea and bacon cobs in the morning restored happy faces. My life has come such a long way especially in the nine years since I started talking about my accident and more recently even more as have chosen to forgive and live a resilient life.

In a nutshell, Resilience: It's okay to reflect on the past but do not dwell there. When you delve into the past too much it's not helpful. It's not about putting things that have happened into boxes, they need to be accepted in order to move on. It's okay to have a little memory about something, just not to put too much focus on it. My life lesson was to not block things out, it may seem to help initially but I'd not dealt with it. By me confronting all of what I had, allowed me to delete it all. When you bury things, it can create a trigger to bring it all back out. My future model is to just imagine that you're driving at night with the headlights on, how far can you see? When you're driving, do you keep worrying on what might be way ahead, or do you just focus on that bit in front of you? To me, your future should be what is in your headlights, that is your present. No-one's future has ever transpired out to be the same as what they imagined it would be.

There's a well-known American motivational speaker, businessman and author, W. Mitchell, that is a burn victim and paraplegic and I think he sums this up perfectly. One of his quotes is, "**Before I was paralyzed there were 10,000 things I could do. Now there are 9,000. I can either dwell on the 1,000 I've lost or focus on the 9,000 I have left**." (W. Mitchell, 2018).

I heard from Dan to say that he was going into hospital for just a couple of weeks. He was having some bone marrow treatment, where they remove his own marrow, perform a new procedure then reinject it. Then he had to be in isolation as he'd be at high risk of infection. After that, he'd be out. The medical care was successful but then he developed sepsis and he sadly died from that in July of this year, 2018. I attended his funeral and on hearing his eulogy that his daughter had written, it was just like listening to Dan. He had brought his family up with the same positive mindset. His daughter Ruth said that she had something to tell me a couple of weeks after the service - she was pregnant. She'd always thought that she couldn't have children and now they were hoping for a boy so they could call him Dan. Thankfully she'd been able to share the amazing news with Dan before he passed, his 3rd grandchild, as he has two from his other daughter Katie. On the service sheet was a lovely photo of him, and after asking his family, I had it made into a picture. It sits on the wall in my office behind my desk and in a weird kind of a way, I feel as though he's still looking over my shoulder. He'd always been very protective, as Ian, a speaker he had originally worked with had died as he had overworked himself. During his 19 years of recovery after his initial diagnosis, he had seen his daughters marry and his grandkids were born. Then more news from Ruth... the scan had revealed it was a boy.

Dan was a true inspiration and I will miss him greatly.

Depression is when you live in the past and anxiety when you're in the future. Learn to stay in the present. When you find yourself slipping, don't beat yourself up, just notice where you are, take some deep breaths and come back to the present. Matt taught me all of this - knowledge is power and once you recognise why you're feeling anxious it really makes a difference. Taking a holistic approach helps me to create balance, to eat better, improve my sleep and indulge in a little bit of meditation. Learning to breathe properly can change your life. Where I am today, reflecting on my life, I am very happy as I know that everything in my past had to happen in that order to be where I am now. What do we measure as success? Financial wealth did not bring me happiness. Success for me is enjoying the things I can do, being proud of what I've achieved and seeing how my new found resilience has had such a positive effect on my family and friends. We've all got challenges, it's how smooth we make that ride.

I can now look on what I've achieved since my accident and especially since I started speaking nine years ago, I have done a parachute jump, drove a rally car, flown a microlight and a glider, completed my HUET training so I could be flown off shore by helicopter to an oilrig, which we think is world first. I have been involved in some of the UK's most prestigious construction and civil projects including being the Safety Ambassador for the *Aircraft Carrier Alliance* who built the UK's new aircraft carriers. I was honoured to be awarded an MBE for services in H&S in the construction industry in 2015. In 2016 a lifetime achievement award from the NWCSG. I was invited to attend a Royal Garden Party for celebrating their centenary, for 7000 people, and I actually got a ticket for the Royal Enclosure with just 50 other guests, I was made an Arch Angel by *RoSPA* the same year. I have made 3 highly regarded safety films with *Outtakes* that are still used by safety trainers today and most recently in September we saw the official launch of my new partnership with Professor Tim Marsh, *Anker & Marsh.* Along with my inspirational talks, we were also offering a full service of training, assessment and consultancy. I knew that this was going to lead onto even greater places and I was very excited for what was to come. The final thing was to write this book which has been an amazing journey for me, tough at times as I have had to look back at old stuff for the purpose of it being written. That in itself, has highlighted several points to me that I have included in my story on these pages.

I now look at the cracks in my life like the gilded cracks on the 'Kintsugi' vase, but this vase is all of us, we all have cracks in our lives but the key thing is the vase might be even nicer with the gold emboss than when it was new and perfect, and even if it isn't, we're back to the focusing on the positives, it's still a nice vase... Each of us should look for a way to cope with traumatic events in a positive way, learn from negative experiences, take the best from them and convince ourselves that exactly these experiences make each person unique. This is the essence of resilience

Before I sign off, I would like to sincerely apologise to my Mum and Dad for all the heartache I have caused you. To Sharon for always just being there. Abbi and Sam, I hope you have good memories of your childhood. Thank you to the rest of my family, friends and everyone who has supported me over the years and to everyone that I did wrong by, it was never my intention.

Jason x

How I came to be using a ghost-writer

The time felt right for me to share my whole story after my nine years of speaking, where I only get the opportunity to share a snapshot of my story. However, as my work schedule is so busy, it wouldn't allow for the time it would take to write a book.

At an event, I attended I was recommended a person that sounded just what I needed, and I proceeded to contact this writer on LinkedIn. We arranged to meet and what drew me was the fact that this person, Samantha Houghton, had experienced trauma also in her past, and after writing her own book, I felt confident that she would understand what I had been through. My only concern about using a ghost-writer was that the voice of the book would not sound like me. However, I need not have worried as the tone and personality of the way the manuscript was written was just like me! Amazing. My daughter, Abbi, could not believe it either.

After a book vision and planning session and a series of interviews in person, my book was written chapter by chapter for me to review over a period of four months. It was tough going at times, revisiting my past but it has also been a cathartic experience which has resulted in this wonderful book you are reading now that I hope to make a difference to those that need it.

Should you wish to contact Samantha, please contact her via email to sam@samanthahoughton.co.uk or visit www.samanthahoughton.co.uk

Contact page

For all bookings contact

Proud2bSafe Ltd

www.p2bs.org

Contact abbi@p2bs.org

Anker & Marsh

www.ankerandmarsh.co.uk

Contact info@ankerandmarsh.com

Free film to view, with special thanks to *Outtakes*

Contact laura.cade@videointeract.co.uk

Proud2bSafe- https://youtu.be/bzadIyKspc4